I'm Just Saying, "It Looks Like Ethnic Cleansing"

(The Gentrification of Harlem)

I'm Just Saying, "It Looks Like ETHNIC CLEANSING"

(The Gentrification of Harlem)

By Dorothy Pitman Hughes

DPH Book Publishing
Jacksonville, Florida

I'M JUST SAYING
"IT LOOKS LIKE ETHNIC CLEANSING"
(The Gentrification of Harlem)
Published by DPH Book Publishing
2708 Caldar Court
Jacksonville, FL 32259
904-386-9703
dorothyhughes02@yahoo.com

Dorothy Hughes, Publisher
Patrice Quinn, Editor
Yvonne Rose, Associate Editor
QualityPress.info, Production Coordinator
The Printed Page, Interior Design & Cover Layout

Copyright © 2012 by Dorothy Pitman Hughes
ISBN #: 978-0-9853641-0-6
Library of Congress Control Number: 2012939532

Dedication

This book is dedicated to Samuel P. Peabody and The Peabody Family.

Sam, I am in awe and filled with gratitude that such grace would unfold in my life as to send me the kinds of help and the kinds of friends that I have been given. You, who are one of the very dearest of friends to me, have made such a difference in my life—especially in the way that you have consistently helped me in my endeavors to make a difference in the lives of others. And your friendship helps me every day to know that we are always—even through adversity—safe in the hands of True Love.

I first heard the Peabody name when your mother, at the age of 72, was arrested in St. Augustine, Florida, where she and a group of other brave Americans had traveled in support of desegregation. She had been arrested for attempting to eat at a segregated restaurant in an integrated group. During that same time, there was a famous photograph taken of the manager of a motel in St. Augustine pouring acid into a swimming pool where black and white children were swimming together. She bravely challenged the KKK and the St. John's legal system when she put her own body in the way of their intended physical abuse of Dr. King, Professor Andrew Young and others. In jail, when it was discovered that she was the mother of the Governor of Massachusetts, Endicott Peabody, she refused to be released until her son was able to come and get Dr. King and his group out along with her. She helped bring the needed attention to the civil rights movement to the world, and President Lyndon Johnson soon passed the American Civil Rights Act of 1964.

Even before then, when I was still young and living in Georgia, I had heard of your sister, Marietta Tree because of her work with Adlai Stevenson and her social consciousness. But also, I thought I had never heard such a pretty name. I thought she must be a beautiful woman and I said to myself, "*When I get to New York, I'd like to meet Marietta Tree.*"

I came to New York, and began the social advocacy work with children and parents on Manhattan's Westside. My efforts had received some coverage in the news media, and I soon received a phone call from Mrs. Marietta Peabody Tree inviting me to lunch at her home across town.

I had organized a daycare program in the living room of my Westside apartment and had no financial means to keep it going. Marietta said she had arranged for the world famous violinist, Isaac Stern (he and his wife Vera were neighbors on the Westside) to give a small concert at her home for me, and her list of friends. That day at lunch, she handed me the key to her home—she would be traveling, and so could not attend, herself—and asked me just to help make sure Mr. Stern didn't scratch her floor when he brought in his equipment. From the concert, donations amounting to $32,000.00 were collected for what became the West 80th Street Daycare Center, and eventually expanded to include the New York City Agency for Child Development.

I didn't even know who you were then, but I could have guessed that you would be as graceful and genuine as your mother and sister. Years later, my friend and eventual speaking partner would say to me, "I know someone you have to meet". And Gloria Steinem introduced me to you.

You immediately embraced my family. My children and I, year after year, attended Christmas Day dinners at your home, where we were truly welcomed by you, your lovely wife, Judith, your daughter, Elizabeth and friends.

You helped me, through the years, with the education of my children, the illnesses of my mom and dad, the mentoring of my grandsons; and now, in giving me the financial assistance that has allowed me to finish this book.

I thank you, your mom, your sister, your wife and daughter for your love, understanding and friendship. Please know you have helped an African American family to reach some of the goals that we aspired to, and we are all dedicated to continue in the tradition of "brotherly love" that you are so distinguished in representing.

From the Pitman Hughes Family to the Peabody Family: Our Love and Thanks.

Dorothy Hughes

Acknowledgements

I humbly thank all the people who helped me to develop and sustain H.O.S., Inc.:

The Former Board of Directors of the Harlem Office Supply, Inc.; the 7000 Shareholders of HOS, Inc.; our legal team; our CPA's, De Pieto, Blum and Company; Samuel Peabody; Susan Eastman; Oprah Winfrey; Gene Kendall; Jay McGovern; Ben Wilson; Joey; James Jackson; Vernon Gibson; Joseph Palmer; Carrie Harris; Gloria Dulan-Wilson; Mel Williams, Tony Jenkins; Rev. Dennis Dillon; Al Pierce; Garfield MacIntyre; Chitra; Yvonne Maddox; Gail V. Leonard; Delilah; Joan H. Bernstein, Gloria Steinem; Susan Taylor; Bob Law; Prof. Luther Seabrook; Bill Tatum; John Beatty; Daisy Laurence; Showman's; My Grandsons Sean William Ridley and Devin Edward Batiste; Beverly Griggsby; Clarence Hughes; My Daughters: Delethia Marvin, Patrice Quinn and Angela Hughes; Hubert Collins; Pat Stevenson; Corinthia Dean; Alma Scott; Jean Berry; Grace Richman; Charlotte Blassingame; Faye Carter; Paul Quinn; Jonas Malmsten; Yvonne Rose; Tony Rose; My Sisters: Mildred Dent; Julia Van Matre; Mary Cunningham and Alice Ridley; Ruby Harris; Ruben Harris; and the late: William Pitman; Ayre Owens; Roger Ridley; Lessie Ridley and Milton Ridley.

Dorothy Hughes

Contents

Foreword by Gloria Dulan-Wilson

I'm just saying: IT LOOKS LIKE ETHNIC CLEANSING to me, too!

When Dorothy Pittman-Hughes told me that she was writing a book, I was totally thrilled. All I could say was "It's about time!"

When she told me title of the book, *It Looks Like Ethnic Cleansing,* I said "Wow! This is going to be deep!" Deep was an understatement. There was so much that had not been dealt with in the saga of how Harlem has fallen into the hands of gentrifiers, and how those who tried to retain it as the Mecca of the Black World, a community of quality, prosperity, and progress, were (and continue to be) driven out. Such a one was Dorothy Pitman-Hughes. She had been on the front line from the very beginning in trying to save Harlem. But, after reading the draft, I knew that she was now ready to reveal her side of the story.

Dorothy and I have been friends for nearly 30 years. From 1984, when I first returned to New York after a nine-year stint of residing in California, to now. I've always said good people always find each other. Thank God one of the many good people in my life turned out to be Dorothy—or Dot, as she is affectionately called.

I had returned to a New York that was struggling to overcome the ravages of a major economic downturn, borne of a callous Republican regime that was bent on moving the financial capital from New York to California. Thank goodness that plan failed miserably. But it left New York at the mercy of prolonged deferred maintenance, decay, rising crime rates, low producing schools, the decimation of manufacturing and other service jobs.

Nevertheless, I was so glad to be back in the Apple, I was willing to tackle whatever the challenge was to never, ever leave the East Coast again. Still, I had been away so long I was totally out of step for the fast pace we commonly call "a New York minute." One of the first people to help me get it together and get back on my feet was Dot.

It was at Northern Lights, an upscale night club on the second floor of the CAV Building on W. 125th Street, between Malcolm X and Fifth Avenues. I hadn't entered the realm of the Black Press, yet, and was trying to reacquaint myself with the New York nightlife I had missed so much. I had come to the club "solo" because someone told me they had good jazz and live entertainment. So there I sat, on a high stool, with my one drink. Dorothy and some other Harlemites were sitting at a table across the room. After I had been there an hour and hadn't moved from the spot, she came over to me, introduced herself, and asked if I was visiting.

When I explained that I had just moved back after a 9-year absence, she invited me to join her and her friends at their table instead of sitting alone. When I hesitated, she said, "We don't bite, and it makes no sense to be by yourself," I followed her to her table. After a few minutes of small talk, I quickly realized that I had made the right decision, and that New Yorkers were still—as I had always bragged on them to be—friendly, unceremonious, and open—if they like you.

The live entertainment turned out to be Dorothy, who got up and sang a few songs, backed up by the band. When she returned to the table, she asked me what I was into. And, since I was still in the throes of getting back into the flow, I really had nothing to speak of. Of course, all that was about to change. I was beginning to realize that I had connected with one of the most dynamic women in Harlem—actually one of the most dynamic Divas on the planet!

Dorothy is truly a force of nature. There is very little that she does not do well, and do to the max. She is not one for half measures. She moves whole soul into any and everything she turns her attention to. And that bode well for Harlem, because she had decided to turn her focus on our village, and make sure that we had everything the rest of New York provided so lavishly for its other neighborhoods.

As she states in *It Looks Like Ethnic Cleansing*: "Harlem has long been viewed as the cultural capital of African Americans." And that's absolutely true. Other communities in other parts of the US both love, envy, and fear Harlem. They try to compete with the talent, intelligence, and energy. But the moment they think they've figured it out, Harlem makes a change, creates a nuance, and the rest of the world has to play catch up all over again.

For Harlemites, especially those born and raised there, Harlem is either a haven or hell, but it's always home. People who have lived outside of New York City for over 30 years still say they're from Harlem (or New York City). There's that sense of pride and belonging that never goes away. It's in our DNA.

In *It Looks Like Ethnic Cleansing*, Dorothy wisely states that "Harlem occupies a strategic place in the national psyche" and was (is) viewed as the cultural capital of African Americans. Harlem is internationally renowned for its people and their contributions to politics, literature, music, dance, sports, and art; it was also viewed as a dangerous place, the "inner-city," the metaphor for urban America, the place where social pathology abounds." I've actually known people who do not go south of 110th Street, or north of 157th. There is an interesting internal boundary that some have hardwired in their system, so that that small community is all there is for them.

For them, a Dorothy Pittman-Hughes was an absolute necessity, because without the resources she brought to the neighborhoods, they would likely continue to subsist without the essential goods and services—Child care facilities; Harlem Office Copy to get stationery, xeroxing, greeting cards and other services that, at that time, did not exist in many local stores.

But Dorothy was more than that: With her talents and skills, she was an entrepreneur, pioneer, leader, activist, mother, grandmother, friend, sister, artist, entertainer, philanthropist, and role model—all in the statuesque frame of a tall, full figured sister who moved through the community with grace and power.

She loves Harlem and loves Black people—not to the exclusion of white people; not in an adversarial manner—no! Dorothy has friends of all races, nationalities, religions, genders, economic standings, educational backgrounds, interests, professions, and leanings. But her first love was for Black people, people of African heritage—descendants of the victims of chattel slavery, and are now struggling in a modern society to overcome educational, social and economic apartheid here in New York City.

Dorothy nailed it when she decided to employ the term "ethnic cleansing" to describe the unrelenting attacks on Harlem's neighborhoods, residents, businesses and housing stock. As she states, "Ethnic Cleansing is a term broadly used to describe all forms of ethnically motivated violence. The planned deliberate removal of a particular ethnic group from a special territory, or forced deportation or population transfer of parts or all of a particular ethnic group, the means used to this end range from the legal to semi-legal to illegal."

That about sums it up in a nutshell. What we have here is a concerted effort to replace Black people who have resided in Harlem since the early 20th century, with whites—now that we've done the hard work of making the community attractive, liveable, fun, convenient, viable—the push is to push African Americans out, and move white Americans in.

It's nothing new. It has happened in many communities throughout the US, and in 2012, continues to be an issue. Some times called gentrification; it boils down to the same thing. It's Plessy v. Ferguson all over again, to wit, "a Black man has no rights that a white man is bound to respect." Be it his home, his community, his business, or even his woman, they all become fair game. However, in the 21st century, there are some more sophisticated methods in play.

"Ethnic cleansing," she states wisely, "according to the 1992 UN General Assembly is a form of GENOCIDE: "…aggressive acts by hostile forces to acquire more territories by force, characterized by a consistent pattern of gross and systematic violations of human rights, a burgeoning refugee population resulting from mass expulsions of defenseless civilians from their homes," as evidenced by overpriced properties, marked up exponentially to make it difficult for low to moderate income families to afford the cost of purchase; coupled with taking over local stores, restaurants and other ancillary services, pricing them so far out of their range of affordability, they are no longer able to remain in their community.

Sound familiar? Think it can't happen in New York City? In the 60's it was called Urban Renewal. Under our breaths we called it "negro removal." It was clear that the intention was to make sure that the people who currently resided in the community would no longer be there. They were characterized as "undesirable;" increased police presence to protect the interlopers, as opposed to secure the residents already residing there.

A master plan, in which none of the current residents have any input, is in place long before the first bulldozer rolls down the street, or via imminent domain, homes that have been the center of the community are condemned to make way for overpriced condominium developments. Think it can't happen, just check out Brooklyn, which has 65 vacant condominium buildings on the foot prints of what used to be primarily Black Communities.

However, Harlem's angst began long before Brooklyn became the target. But in some instances, it was a gradual, almost underground process, for fear of causing reprisals from the residents.

A consummate business woman and Harlem community leader, Dorothy was instrumental in helping design the original federally funded Urban Empowerment Zone and Enterprise Committee Program for the *Revitalization of Harlem.* It was introduced into legislation by Congressman Charles E. Rangel in 1993, while Bill Clinton was still

President of the United States. It was one of the most comprehensive programs yet, designed to completely turn Harlem around, upgrade the community, businesses, educational facilities, and provide opportunities for local entrepreneurs to start, own and run their own businesses and expand much needed goods and services. The designated area was granted $100 million in federal dollars.

During the initiation of the program, David N. Dinkins was mayor of New York City; Mario Cuomo was Governor of the State of New York, and of course Bill Clinton was President of the United States—all democrats.

However, in 1995, by the time all the details had been hashed out, and the legislation had gone into effect, Rudolf Giuliani was mayor, George Pataki was governor, Randy Daniels was Secretary of State, all Republican. Whatever effect and influence Congressman Charles Rangel may have had in Congress, meant very little when it came to it implementation. You might say they flipped the script on Harlem; waited until all the funds had been allocated, and shifted everything to cronies of the the governor, the mayor and others who had no compunction about diverting the funds from locally owned Black businesses to corporations who had no need of the funds.

Governor Pataki and Mayor Giuliani each matched the federal commitment for a total of $300 million, the sum originally allocated to empower the existing community, in large part by providing loans, tax breaks and assistance to the area businesses. Instead, gentrification was the result of the Empowerment Zone Plan.

The proud single mother of three beautiful daughters, Patrice, Delethia and Angela, Dorothy has always been a positive role model for them, as well as the rest of the children in the community—including my own daughters and my son. She displays a deep sense of ethics and compassion regardless of who she's dealing with. Concerned about making sure they learn from her example, she was motivated to document her experiences so they would not have to wonder why she "spent so many years doing what they have seen me do. I want them to know that I know I have been discriminated against; and that although I have suffered under the burden of racism, sexism and classism, I have chosen to stand up for our rights as Americans."

And stand up she did. She stood when the rest of the community either turned a blind eye, or was too frightened to make a move. She stood and when there was something she didn't know, or understand, she made it her business to learn from the experts, and in turn teach it to others.

Dorothy thrives on challenges, but even more so revels in winning— especially when it's a win-win situation. And while she'd prefer not to operate under adversarial conditions, she didn't back down. A trait that others have hopefully picked up from being in her company. I know I sure have.

The problem, however, with women of strength and vision, is that others are more than willing to dump their problems on her, and stand back and watch her handle it, rather than offering their support. On the other hand there are also those who are threatened by her strength, and will do what they can to thwart her efforts, sabotage her plans, and circumvent the plans that would have made it possible for all to live in and thrive in Harlem.

It Looks Like Ethnic Cleansing, takes you through her struggle to save Harlem from gentrification. For many of you, what you read will be of no surprise to you, but an affirmation of what you had already suspected to be true. Dorothy not only gives you the inside information to verify your suspicions, but the ammunition you need to prevent further incursions on the freedom so many worked so hard to establish.

Some of the revelations will make you furious. Other passages will totally blow you away. The extent to which adversaries have gone to thwart the development of a cohesive Black Harlem community is actually not new. There are enough heroes and villains to go around, locally and nationally; Black and white.

Dorothy was tireless and relentless in her drive to wake Harlem up. She was not a nine-to-five lady. That concept totally escapes Dorothy. Having worked with her as late as 4:00AM, either at Harlem Office Copy, or at her brownstone home, completing a community project, putting together flyers, writing proposals, she didn't stop until it was done. Many a midnight oil burned conducting research, organizing a fundraiser, setting up a networking program; coordinating a business or networking tour. There were no computers, cell phones, email hadn't really reached primacy—so everything was hands on. There were so many resources that were not available in the Harlem of the 80's and 90's. Dorothy worked diligently to provide access for struggling business owners.

But, while she was focused on opening opportunities, taking special courses on her own; being tutored by those who were inside Wall Streeters so she could then pass the info on to her fellow business owners; there were others just as devoted to closing those doors.

Many people placed in positions of trust and responsibility for implementing the empowerment zone programs, were culpable in undermining the program, so that the benefits went to everyone but the local merchants, business owners, and residents of Harlem. No doubt they were well paid.

Dorothy refers to it as "slaveholders putting a whip in the hands of a slave and demanding that he beat his mama." How graphic, and how accurate! She invites you to "Have a look at some of our political leaders and see if they are not doing the same to their constituents" blocking the ability to develop economic empowerment was to cut off the life's blood of the Black community.

A master plot was executed with deadly accuracy. As Dorothy states, without economic empowerment there would not be social or political freedom. It was possible to do business with a bank, but not get a loan for your business or to purchase your home from that very same bank. It was possible for a Black entrepreneur to be relegated to mom and pop status, but to get no support or assistance if s/he wanted to step outside the narrow parameter they'd put him in, and expand or enhance his or her business.

Generally, the whip holders were either officers of a church, the not-for-profit organizations, or want-to-be politicians, or just anyone suffering from the "Willie Lynch Syndrome" and well versed in the fine art of divide and conquer. In Harlem, it was all of the above.

At the point when Harlem businesses thought salvation had finally arrived and all they had worked for was finally bearing fruit, they FLIPPED THE SCRIPT. A new regime had taken the helm; an insidious crew that had watched while all this played out, and sat back on their haunches, ready to snatch victory away from Harlem, its business owners and residents.

It was a surreal moment at the Adam Clayton Powell, Jr. State office building in the heart of Harlem, when the ceremony was set to take place that would bring the Empowerment Zone to Harlem and the Bronx.. Black business owners, elected officials—including David Paterson, Congressman Charles Rangel, Assemblymember Keith Wright, among others, were there symbolically. It was clear that the Republicans had landed and taken over the entire process. It had been conjectured that the whole ceremony was to be canceled. However, they obviously felt it was necessary to rub our faces in their victory. Imagine a state and a city with a Democratic majority, having both a Republican mayor and a governor now deciding the fate of one of the most comprehensive public benefit programs ever enunciated. The $300 million on the table, allocated to help Black and Latino businesses, was now in the hands of people who had absolutely no interest or intention in keeping the tenets of the Empowerment Zone legislation. That money never found its way to the businesses it was intended to help.

As a member of the Black press there to cover the event, I was attacked verbally by one Pataki's female staff from Albany, who insisted that I could not take pictures. Her hostility and rudeness , along with those of her associates toward Harlemites, was evident in both word and deed.

Congressman Rangel was initially not allowed to sit on the podium with the other Republican officials. Members of WISE ("Women Initiating Self Empowerment") were relegated to the back rows of the already packed State Office Building main room, that barely holds 100 people comfortably. {Oddly enough, when the building was designed, no one saw fit to include an auditorium large enough to accommodate the community. It was recently "remodeled," and there still isn't one—go figure}.

As Dorothy stated, "African American business owners were happily welcoming The Empowerment Zone, as it was portrayed by our congressman and others. We were herded into meeting halls to hear of the wonderful things that were to happen in Harlem. And then we watched our African American leaders give support and loans to made-up (fabricated) 'Harlem' businesses, and to corporations and entities like Staples, Foot Locker, Disney and Tribeca Films -- as they carried out the plan, which, I'm just saying… looks like Ethnic Cleansing."

I totally concur, it definitely looked like ethnic cleansing to me too. Harlem had been invaded by occupying forces that were to remain in effect for the next 13 years. From that point forward, if you were not part of the favored party, you operated on the margins. Whatever gains had been made were quickly reversed, siphoned off, and given to the highest bidder, or political cronies.

It was a hard lesson for Dorothy and the women of WISE. Though she persevered in her efforts to bring about economic empowerment, she didn't realize at the time that their opponents were playing a high stakes game of "keep away." She states "I struggled and made the transition to Harlem businesswoman. And just when I thought I had "arrived", I quickly learned that economically, politically and socially I was nothing but a sharecropper on 125th Street, Harlem, New York." She further states: "We began to notice a trend that seemed grossly unfair: we put money in the banks but we were not given loans. We had done all the dirty work, and they reaped the benefits of our labor. I now understand that that was the plan all along."

Throughout the book Dorothy points out how Harlemites have been routinely undermined in their effort to maintain their businesses. How businesses, such as Copeland's, that had been a mainstay for over 60 years, were callously undermined by the new handlers of the Empowerment Zone. It was the beginning of what we see as the gentrification of today's Harlem. Businesses decimated in the name of "progress." Bogus African American businesses were set up to manipulate the closings of legitimate African American-owned business. Dorothy invites you to examine who the current owners of those businesses are, "and follow the trail of who is the leadership now; you can track to the new ownership. Pitting one Black business against another, and then, when they're ready, that business is forced out of business and supplanted with a white owned company."

If ever there was a champion for Harlem, it was Dorothy Pitman-Hughes. Not to be thwarted by the fact that Empowerment Zone funds had been circumvented, she came up with another method to help business owners obtain much needed funding. She was the first Black woman to sell stock in her business, and teach others how to do the same. She called it going from Share cropping to Share Holding.

It was probably the reason Rolanda Watts decided to feature her on her talk show "*Rolanda*" (a/k/a The *RO Show*), right after Whoopie Goldberg starred in the 1996 movie *"The Associate."* Many of the tactics employed in that movie, had already been employed by Dorothy. Watts had correctly identified Dorothy as an example of what an intelligent, accomplished, creative Black woman had to go through in order to compete with mainstream white businesses. When she came back from the taping to find her business, Harlem Office Supply, had been padlocked, allegedly for back taxes, she made a few polite phone calls, and an apology was forthcoming for having made an "error." It was official, Dorothy was a target. She was in their gun sights. She stood between their steam roller tactics and their goal of subjugating Harlem to their will.

More than just a historical account, *It Looks Like Ethnic Cleansing* is a must read for anyone concerned about the future of Harlem. The future of Black communities everywhere. For those who think "Ethnic Cleansing" can't happen here." Look around you. It already has.—GDW

Gloria Dulan-Wilson is a feature writer and photo journalist, who focuses on issues of concern to Black People. Having written for *The Daily Challenge News, The New York Beacon, Metro Exchange*, and her own blog, www.gloriadulanwilson.blogspot.com/ Eclectically Black News, for nearly 30 years, she considers herself the "Partisan Press." She has interviewed hundreds of political figures, artists all stripes; as well as community leaders and unsung heroes. She was named the "Phenomenal Woman Writer of 2010" by *Our Times Press*.

Introduction

As defined in Wikipedia, "Gentrification refers to the changes that result when wealthier people ("gentry") acquire or rent property in low income and working class communities. Consequent to gentrification, the average income increases and average family size decreases in the community. This results in the displacement of the poorer native residents of the neighborhood, who are unable to pay increased rents, house prices, and property taxes".

So, if Gentrification refers to "the changes that result", what term refers to the causes of those changes? How, and why did the actions that caused the resulting changes occur? What term best describes those?

I'm just saying: *IT LOOKS LIKE ETHNIC CLEANSING.*

"Ethnic Cleansing" is a term broadly used to describe all forms of ethnically motivated violence. Defined as "the planned deliberate removal of a particular ethnic group from a special territory", or "forced deportation or population transfer of parts or all of a particular ethnic group", the means used to this end range from the legal to semi-legal to illegal.

The idea in ethnic cleansing is "to get people to move". Wikipedia records that the academic discourse considers both ethnic cleansing and genocide as existing in a spectrum of assaults on ethnic racial groups; genocide being a subset of "murderous ethnic cleansing".

I first heard the term "Ethnic Cleansing" when I was a child. German Jews were being killed, and my father went to war.

In the 1990s, during the wars in Croatia and Bosnia (the former Yugoslavia) the term was again heard regularly in the news. There was a large outcry by people in the international community for the U.S. to intervene. President Clinton eventually deployed US peacekeepers, and the leaders of those actions were brought to trial as war criminals. But not before an entire group of people were "removed" in one way or another.

In 1992, the United Nations General Assembly deemed ethnic cleansing to be a form of genocide stating:

> "...*aggressive acts by the Serbian and Montenegrin forces to acquire more territories by force, characterized by a consistent pattern of gross and systematic violations of human rights, a burgeoning refugee population resulting from mass expulsions of defenseless civilians from their homes... in pursuit of the abhorrent policy of "ethnic cleansing", which is a form of genocide"*...

Ethnic Cleansing is a political tactic. Ethnic Cleansing removes the condition for potential and actual opposition by removing the ethnic group from the community. It is a way of ensuring that *total* control is put in place over a people. I present this term as a possible descriptive of what has recently taken place in Harlem, New York.

As a businesswoman and community leader in Harlem, I helped design the government funded Urban Empowerment Zone and Enterprise Committee Program for the Revitalization of Harlem. Congressman Charles E. Rangel introduced the legislation to Congress in 1993. The designated area was granted $100 million in federal grants. Governor Pataki and Mayor Giuliani each matched the federal commitment; there was a total of $300 million, which was to empower the existing community, in large part by providing loans, tax breaks and assistance to the area businesses. It did not.

And so, as a historical record, I give you my first-hand account of the process that is resulting in the gentrification of Harlem; a process that I can only describe as the planned deliberate removal of parts, or all of a particular ethnic group from a special territory.

Chapter One

Freedom, Another Introduction

Long before I moved to Harlem, I set a goal to ensure, and enjoy my full citizenship. I always believed that I could openly pursue educational opportunities, buy a home in any area I could afford, create and own a business, have the same rights as other Americans to the full use of the banking system, enjoy the protection of the legal system, and choose my political and religious direction. I have continuously engaged in human rights activities that I believed would ensure this goal being met for myself and others. To date I am aware of over 1,000 news articles, several radio and television interviews, and 16 books, among other documents, where my efforts have been recorded.

I feel the need to write this book so that my children won't have to wonder why I've spent so many years doing what they have seen me do. I want them to know that I know I have been discriminated against; and that although I have suffered under the burden of racism, sexism and classism, I have chosen to stand up for our rights as Americans.

So many Americans seem to believe that we, who are African American and victims of racism, are at fault for what we experience. They seem surprised that we would talk about racism, sexism and classism today, in what is thought of as a post-racist America. Those of this generation who believe that this "democracy" is not overrun with racism, classism and sexism need to make some immediate historic checks.

Have you heard or read the accounts of slaveholders putting a whip in the hands of a slave and demanding that he beat his mama? Have a look at some of our political leaders and see if they are not doing the same to their constituents.

We are not in a post-racist America, we are still building "black" ghettos and poor "white" ghettos, and actively working to racially divide ethnic and cultural groups. Before Africans were enslaved in America the terms "black" and "white" were not even in the vernacular. The world saw itself as a world of different nations, ethnicities and cultures. The whole concept of social and political division along "racial" lines was born out of a desire to maintain a slave state. But With the abolition of slavery, America promised to now see itself as a nation of different ethnicities with the common "culture" of democracy. Why do we see and hear these concepts of racial division being constantly promoted? And why are African American communities, and the resources we create still constantly under siege?

Sharecropping

The practice of slavery was abolished, only to be followed by the practice of sharecropping. Early on in the years of my involvement in the struggle for civil rights, I had not completely understood the economic value involved for those who control the system. I heard what was being said, but my focus was on staying alive. I had not yet realized that without economic empowerment I would not have social or political freedom.

Since I began writing this book, we have elected the first African American President of the United States. He ran on a promise of "Change", and in spite of much resistance, he has managed to accomplish some significant changes in our government and the lives of US citizens. On April 5, 2012 President Barack Obama signed a new Bill entitled the "Jumpstart Our Business Startups Act" or "JOBS Act". This Bill essentially calls for the very same thing I worked so hard to accomplish in Harlem, and was basically run out of town for, through the efforts of then State Attorney General and subsequently Governor, Eliot Spitzer, and others. If you or anyone you know has interest in using this new JOBS Act to jumpstart your businesses and our American economy; or to economically empower those who have been systematically left out, I recommend you read this book and share it, as I believe it will give you invaluable insight and wisdom for your endeavor. It provides a clear description of the principles involved in creating and sustaining a healthy and just economic system; and as a first-hand account of my struggle to do that, it will help you avoid the pitfalls, which unfortunately may very well await you.

I intend to be with you in continuing (through this Bill and otherwise) to do everything I can to help socially, politically and economically empower African Americans and all people who have been injured by the injustices of racism, sexism and classism in our country. Let this book be your "handbook" as you endeavor to understand and work for social, political and economic "Change".

Chapter Two

Harlem

In the period I lived on the mid Westside of Manhattan, I started a daycare center from my apartment; and worked as an organizer, co-founding NYC's agency for Child Development, which today cares for over 700,000 children daily. I was also working with political representatives to create alternatives to welfare legislation; creating job training programs, food programs and securing education, good work and careers for literally thousands of people.

My work led the transformation of a "troubled", ethnically and economically diverse neighborhood of African Americans, immigrant families from Europe, South America and the Caribbean; single, and married working mothers and fathers, and families on welfare, all butted up against some of the wealthiest people in America, into a thriving community of neighbors.

My daughters received early childcare and education in my day care center, attended a progressive community school we set up in the neighborhood, and later the public schools we worked with to ensure proper care and education for our children there. They participated in after school and summer programs I organized in order to care for children while their parents worked, and to expose them to the arts, culture, and nature.

I had worked nationally in the Civil Rights movement with Malcolm X and Dr. Martin Luther King, and with The Deacons, SNCC and other organizations. We had seen new legislation passed to protect African Americans' rights as citizens. And I had helped to create a real pathway locally for African Americans and other poor and disenfranchised families to start to reach for "the American dream" of prosperity.

I was happy, and I believed that I had really "made it" when I was able to buy a beautiful brownstone and move my family to Harlem. My husband and ex-husband and I, along with our daughters, worked to renovate it; knocking out walls and blow-torching and scraping years of paint off the mahogany doors and window frames and the 6 carved fireplace mantles. I planted two trees in front and a rose bush in the back garden. I was delighted when I furnished the rooms—each of them with ceilings twelve feet high—with wonderful furniture and art. I was especially pleased with each of my three daughters' bedrooms, where they would sit at their desks in serenity, with space and beauty all around them, do their homework or daydream. They could sleep restfully each night and awaken to days that with so much invested in them, could only get brighter for them.

Harlem, I soon learned, lacked many of the services that had been available to me as a resident of Greenwich Village and the mid Westside of Manhattan. I needed to copy some documents, so I went to someone's office at The Hotel Theresa, where I was able to make copies at twenty-five cents each. Then I began to put together a plan to open a copy center. I knew that if I had a need for such a service there must be others with that same need.

In the summer of 1985 the first Harlem Copy Center was opened on Lenox Avenue between 124th and 125th Streets. The business was launched successfully; with 8 full time employees and four youth, who worked and trained after school. We offered, as part of the services: copying, typing, printing and tutoring. I had struggled, and made the transition to Harlem businesswoman. And just when I thought I had "arrived", I quickly learned that economically, politically and socially, I was nothing but a sharecropper on 125th Street, Harlem, New York.

Chapter Three

A Special Territory

Harlem has long been viewed as the cultural capital of African Americans. As an African American community, it had begun as a "ghetto", the creation of which, by the way, is cited as one of the tactics used in "ethnic cleansing".

It had experienced the famous Harlem Renaissance that influenced the entire world, and it existed then and now as a place of both opportunity and problems. And despite years of neglect and systematic exclusion from the mainstream economy, its residents and entrepreneurs worked undaunted and without reparations to protect and uplift our beloved community.

At one time there were even visions of developing international trade between and among "third world" countries through its Trade Center. In earlier years the First Black Congressman from Harlem, Adam Clayton Powell, Jr., who was also the Pastor of Abyssinian Baptist Church and lived and based his operations in Harlem, was the political arm of the National movement for the empowerment of African American citizens, and made great strides. In the 1960s Governor Nelson Rockefeller built the Harlem State Office Building, later named for Congressman Powell. The landmark Apollo Theatre, which had fallen into decline in the 1960s and 1970s, was revived in 1983, when former Manhattan Borough President, the Honorable Percy Sutton purchased the building, and his Inner City Broadcasting firm began broadcasting the national television show, "Showtime at the Apollo" from it. Also in the 1980's, John Beatty reopened the world-famous Cotton Club.

In addition to being a place of international and historic cultural significance and still an attraction for tourists, Harlem has prime physical attributes: its location in relation to the rest of the city, New Jersey and upstate NY, its three bridges, its hundreds of brownstones and beautiful apartment buildings with marble lobbies—once boarded up, and now being advertised and sold to the "gentry" as "Deluxe Pre-War" condos—the Harlem and Hudson Rivers, the riverside and inland parks, churches, hotels, hospitals and school buildings and the campuses of The City College of NY and Columbia University, among other institutes of higher learning.

I came across this assessment of the demographics and atmosphere of Harlem just before the arrival of the Empowerment Zone. I don't know who wrote it or where it was published, but I include it here as an accurate description of our community at that time:

> *A new dynamic in Harlem neighborhoods was the mix of new immigrants and African Americans. The new residents came mainly from Mexico, the Dominican Republic, Korea, Guatemala, Honduras, Belize, Senegal, and the Ivory Coast. Though there were some apparent similarities between the immigrants and Black Americans, there were some critical linguistic and cultural differences. These differences had the effects, both of creating ethnic tensions, and of stimulating growth while producing vitality. However, the combination of racial discrimination and cycles of economic boom and bust placed many African American and Puerto Rican residents on the fringe of the mainstream economy with their immigrant neighbors. The infusion of African trade in the arts and crafts, Puerto Rican and Dominican acumen in commerce, and African American continued contemporary creation of new cultural forms, combined to make Harlem one of the most vibrant urban areas in the world.*

If Harlem was the black cultural capital of the world, then the Apollo Theater was its State House, whose restoration epitomized the determination of a community to reclaim its heritage. Likewise, the redevelopment of the Latino/Caribbean marketplace, La Marqueta, was a cherished symbol of neighborhood identity for El Barrio. It was a signature of place. The retail explosion along upper Broadway by the Dominicans brought new energy to the New York City economy. In physical terms, high density and pressures of overcrowding were manifested in the neighborhoods of West Harlem and Washington Heights. In Central and East Harlem neighborhoods, large-scale housing abandonment resulted in lower densities. *Nevertheless, if there was a problem of overcrowding, this condition was accompanied by high rates of city ownership of vacant and occupied housing,* as well as concentration of public housing. In the high density neighborhoods of West Harlem and Washington Heights, retail goods and services were often plentiful, but poorly diversified and distributed. In neighborhoods of high abandonment rates in Harlem, retail services were inadequate and in some cases, non-existent. In East Harlem there was a mix of concentrated and scarce retail services.

Harlem occupied a strategic place in the national psyche. Harlem was viewed as the cultural capital of African Americans, internationally renowned for its people and their contributions to politics, literature, music, dance, sports, and art; it was also viewed as a dangerous place, the "inner-city," the metaphor for urban America, the place where social pathology abounds.

Chapter Four

Doing Business In Harlem

B ecause the people of Harlem had heard of my advocacy for the community, they soon started to come to the store to speak with me. From that came the Business Network Sessions, which were held at the Cotton Club on the first Thursday of each month. There was an open invitation to struggling entrepreneurs. We helped each other provide good service, while we created support systems to maintain and grow our businesses.

Our respect for each other and the hope we had gained from the civil rights and women's rights movements helped us build our businesses. I was able to move to 125th Street, where we expanded, and became Harlem Office Supply, Inc. There was no other office supply store in Harlem. With our becoming advocates for each other, our businesses were growing. We were now in the position to invest more in them, but we were not able to get loans from the banks.

We put money in the banks but we were not given loans. We hired people, we trained workers; and we contributed to churches, politicians, social programs and projects for third world countries. We paid for breakfast for the man who came past our stores announcing he was hungry, but when contracts were given for bids on products used in our schools, hospitals, universities, political offices or local corporate businesses and city programs, African Americans were consistently blocked from bidding for contracts.

If City College, Columbia University, the hospitals, the banks and the schools in Harlem had each purchased 1% of their monthly supply of Hammermill Copy Paper from Harlem Office Supply, Inc., it would have brought several thousands of dollars a year to the local, small business of a resident, neighbor and fellow businessperson; creating training, jobs, and income, and untold social and political value for the people of that community.

I spent thousands of dollars trying to get a contract with these institutions, for any of the products and services I provided. I tried to get small and large contracts for printing, only to learn that I could not compete with the group who always won the bid. Their printing was being done in prisons, where slavery is legal. The institutional contracts were going to a company called Pride, which presently also contracts with the government, and with popular clothing companies. The fathers of the youth that I was trying to hire were doing their printing work in prison for 6 cents an hour.

I fought for 14 years to sell supplies to a contracting company building schools in Harlem. I was finally awarded a contract by the Board of Education, who sent a letter to the Contractor stating that they'd approved and cleared my business to receive a $30,000 contract to supply the project from start to finish.

This is how I found out that I had won the contract:

I began to receive monthly requests from the building contractor for one case of toilet paper. When I went to the site to see if I could convince the contractor to order more of my products and services, such as printing, copying, and office supplies, I met the young, African American single mom who worked for the company and had been instructed to order the toilet paper from me. I left without a contract, but in the short time I was there, I had made a friend of sorts.

The young woman told me later that she could see in that brief meeting what I was about. And so, after she was fired, she came to me for help. And she told me how it was that I had come to be filling such a strange monthly order. The company had received its instruction to order $30,000 in supplies from Harlem Office Supply over the duration of the project; they had instructed the young woman to order one case of toilet paper from H.O.S. each month in order to generate an invoice so they could show a purchase; and then they changed the figures on the invoices. I was told the $30,000 contract was given to the son of the contractor.

I asked the young woman why she hadn't told me earlier. She said she was afraid she'd lose her job.

Chapter Five

The Empowerment Zone

I first became aware of the Empowerment Zone concept and legislation in this way: I received a call from a person referred to me by someone I consider one of my best friends. The caller, George Dwight, asked if I could be of assistance to his friend Ron Wigginton and his partner from Land Studio in California, who would be coming to Harlem to look at it in relation to the development of a plan called "Vision Harlem". In order to plan for the future of Harlem they would have to really see Harlem – and they wanted entrée to the area without being seen as "integrationists". "So, Dorothy, can you help? Your friend said if anyone can show us the real deal, you can". And so I became a paid consultant for what I later learned was a study of Harlem as a possible Empowerment Zone. The draft illustration of Vision Harlem was completed in 1994.

As we traveled throughout Harlem, we saw the decay of Harlem's infrastructure. In every area where there were concentrations of poor people we saw a lack of sanitation and garbage pick up, substance abuse and trafficking, an intense police presence with more ticketing of cars than in other residential areas of the city, and many homeowners and businesses being ticketed for the constant accumulation of garbage outside their doors due to the lack of sanitation service. We saw a distinct absence of African American ownership and under-funding and underdevelopment of African American business, as the modus operandi remained in the "sharecropping" model. We documented over 1,000 street vendors on 125th Street from 1st Avenue to Broadway. On Wednesdays we saw the real owners of the street goods—which were sold mostly by Africans—come to 125th street, open their folding chairs, collect their money from the vendors and then get back in their cars, taking the money back to their communities.

With these two men, I gained entrance to certain places that I would otherwise have been barred from. We met with heads of corporations, universities and other organizations, and with the bar association. We met during the day with community groups and over dinner, in downtown hotels with corporate heads.

This was the first time I'd heard of the "information and communications superhighway"—the Internet and email. The federal government was involved in a process of innovation. Jobs would be different, and the way people did business would change. George, his friend and their company were applying to the federal government to outline a plan for Harlem that would put Harlem residents in play in the coming new age of technology and business. Their work was part of a bid for the contract to be the ones to design the plan that the federal government would implement.

We worked together over a period of several months, working many evenings over dinner at my house; talking about the problems that existed in Harlem, and how to solve them. They were looking to design a plan that would create economic empowerment "from the bottom up". My work, and outlook as a feminist and civil rights worker gave them some insight to understand how to do it; the principles of it, what our resources were, what our needs were, and what stood in our way.

Their vision included widening certain city streets, changing bus routes and many other improvements to the physical and service infrastructure. And their plan for funding and creating local business and partnerships with larger corporations was inclusive of every ethnic group in the area. Their vision in all areas of the plan linked the communities and supported more ethnically diverse living and working environments.

George and his partner did not get the contract for the design of the empowerment plan, but one project that originated from our discussions, and reflects the vision for the ethnic diversity of their plan, did get built. In the early 90's I worked on the project to build the 125th Street Mart, across the street from the Apollo Theatre. The existence of the Mart allowed for the street vendors to move indoors as well as for artists, craftspeople, and micro-businesses such as hair braiding, manicures, tailoring, and specialty stores to exist and serve the community and the economy. It relieved the sidewalks of crowding and alleviated tensions between the police department and Harlem business owners, residents, and the newest immigrants to the area.

Chapter Six

The Plan

The Empowerment Zone and Enterprise Committees Act of 1993 was a government program to set up an Empowerment Zone in Harlem and The Bronx, as well as other areas throughout the nation. The plan called for a ten year demonstration that through its funding, the EZ communities could sustain the economic and social empowerment of their people. It was to provide Harlem and South Bronx residents with a chance to take their future into their own hands by putting jobs and economic development at the core of community revitalization. It was to be a comprehensive program, including plans for the revitalization of the human and physical resources in EZ neighborhoods.

It was understood that in 1993 the Federal government recognized and sought to remedy the problem of non-capitalization of minority-owned businesses in rural and inner city communities. Legislation was passed to establish Federal Empowerment Zones that focused directly upon minority lending, tax relief for federal, state and local projects impacting on minority hiring, state wage credits and employment opportunities, relocation programs, business resources and investment service centers— all for the purpose of providing a vehicle for inclusion in the American Dream for those who have been systemically left out.

The EZ published statements like, "The EZ will be a *safe* and *secure* community in *reality* and *perception*. The change in the physical environment and economic success will restore *pride* in the *culture* of the residents and will *increase* safety for *all who work in, live in, or visit* Harlem. Large and small-scale businesses were to "co-exist without conflict". The economy was to be diverse. New business partnerships and ownership structures were to be created, in which the economic interests of employees would be at the forefront; there was to be accessibility and availability of capital for our small businesses. The vision linked a flexible system of employment and training to the continuing education of employees. And it was promised that we, the Harlem community, would play a major role in planning and designing this system.

"The EZ journal" printed this quote from President Clinton:

> *The spirit we bring to our work will make the difference. We must be committed to the pursuit of opportunity for all Americans and we must be committed to a new kind of government, not to solve all our problems for us but to give our people the tools they need to make the most of their own lives.*

Alongside it, this quote from Vice President Al Gore:

> *We need to create a climate where families can flourish and hope can blossom.*

The government had recognized what we in these communities have long understood; that there is clearly a need for such a program on inclusion. African American homeowners and would-be homeowners, and large and small African American-owned businesses have experienced redlining and economic discrimination by financial institutions across the country since African Americans were first deemed citizens of the United States. As a result of the stated intentions of the Empowerment Zone, whole new models for revitalizing, building and sustaining Harlem's physical and social infrastructure could be built.

Chapter Seven

WISE

I soon decided that it was important that as one of Harlem's African American, female business owners, I should be on the EZ's Economic Empowerment Planning Committee. Like so many other struggling business owners, I was suffering to keep my business afloat. In Harlem transformation had been a daily process since the assurance of the Empowerment Zone funding.

Harlem's African American entrepreneurs, who for years, struggled to create our businesses and train and hire residents; and many of whom had invested lifetimes in the economy of Harlem were being forced out of business as new businesses were coming in. The landlords, the banks, the political leaders, and businesspeople all over the country were now aware that Harlem was promised and poised to receive an infusion of $300 Million dollars. Harlem was experiencing radical demographic changes fast, which could be very hard to reverse, especially if our presence was diminished.

I was an active member of a women's group, The Women's Action Alliance, downtown, but we needed an action group in Harlem. I hosted a meeting of 12 women and we got together to form a group called W.I.S.E. ("Women Initiating Self Empowerment"). The new organization included: Beulah Tuten, Ann Wells, Ms. Georgia (of Georgie's Donuts) and Sandra Sam, among others—all entrepreneurs who joined W.I.S.E. to help press for equal access to loans for women.

We needed to build a liaison with the managers of Harlem and the Empowerment Zone. If dollars were going to come into Harlem then we wanted to be a part of it and if we were not a part of it, I was definitely going to go to Washington to ask the President to lift the economic embargo against African-American women in Harlem.

I was asked to represent the women of W.I.S.E., and we were eventually able to get me placed on the EZ's Small Business Committee, from which data would be gathered and generated to present to the organizing committees of the EZ and to the banks. We would assess the specific needs of the small business community for our involvement in carrying out the revitalization of Harlem for its residents. In an effort to ensure fair treatment, we began to insist that a woman be appointed to a position of real power in the EZ.

By this time, we had a new President, George W. Bush. The democratic Governor, Andrew Cuomo had been replaced by Governor George Pataki, and Rudolf Giuilani was now Mayor of New York. Many of the original "team" of representatives who had been supportive of the Empowerment Zoning of Harlem, and instrumental in passing the legislation, were no longer in place.

There had definitely been a regime change. Writer Gloria Dulan Wilson and I both attended the presentation of the legislation at the State Office Building in Harlem. In fact she covered the event for the Daily Challenge, a well-known daily newspaper in New York. We discussed how hostile this new group was to Congressman Rangel and all of the Democratic Party that had attended the announcement. They originally had planned not to include Congressman Rangel and others, but did so because he was still the Congressman of that area. The Republican team came into the Adam Clayton Powell State Office Building with such a vengeance. They were very noticeably rude.

Giuliani, who has since made an attempt to run for President, did a neighborhood sweep of vendors, singling out those who had been instrumental in working with the community. Some of the vendors were able to go into the 125th Street Mart for a few months, but then the Mayor and his crew completely closed down the Mart.

Contracts from empowerment zone dollars were given right away to assist white owned businesses and the African American owned businesses were passed over.

Gloria reminded me recently of a meeting held by Essence Magazine for "Essence Week" to discuss the upcoming EZ. Harlem leaders, including Basil Patterson and Congressman Rangel were on the panel. I questioned why there were no women on the panel, and why there were no African American business owners on the planning committee.

We brought these problems to the attention of those we considered our leaders but our politicians had joined with the Mayor, the Governor and Bush. They killed years of efforts by Kermit Eady (Black United Fund), Lorraine Hale (Hale House), Harlem Office Supply Inc., Shange Sikhula (The Record Shack) and many others.

Chapter Eight

Racism, Sexism and Classism

Deborah Wright became President and CEO of the Upper Manhattan EZ Development Corporation (UMEZ). She was African American, and she was a woman, but it's culture that counts. The question is, are people operating within and from a culture of democracy or a culture of racism, sexism and classism? Deborah Wright did not seem to be a friend of the African American owned businesses and neither did Randy Daniels, Pataki's overseer.

I recently spoke to a group of law students. I was asked simply to speak about whatever I had to say to them. I told them, since I wasn't given a subject, or parameters for my speech, that all I could think to give them in the way of advice was to: "Try to be a whole person." Harriet Tubman, in an interview she gave near the end of her life stated, "I could have freed more people, if they knew they were slaves."

Classism in the African American communities of America is almost equal in its prevalence to racism in America. Some in the generations of African Americans who have benefited most from the civil rights movements think that they earned the opportunities to be in these positions on their own. It seems they feel that they are so much smarter than those of us who fought real battles for their freedom. They seem to think that, by virtue of having been educated in schools we fought to give them access to, they have "earned" for themselves the rights and privileges they enjoy.

I want to tell you here, about what is known as the "Willie Lynch Syndrome", and where the symptoms and phenomena that constitute this destructive syndrome began. What follows is a speech given by Willie Lynch, a European settler, to his fellow slaveholders in 1712:

Gentlemen, I greet you here on the bank of the James River in the year of our Lord one thousand seven hundred and twelve. First, I shall thank you, the gentlemen of the Colony of Virginia, for bringing me here. I am here to help you solve some of your problems with slaves. Your invitation reached me on my modest plantation in the West Indies, where I have experimented with some of the newest and still the oldest methods for control of slaves. Ancient Rome would envy us if my program is implemented. As our boat sailed south on the James River, named for our illustrious King, whose version of the Bible we cherish, I saw enough to know that your problem is not unique. While Rome used cords of wood as crosses for standing human bodies along its highways in great numbers, you are here using the tree and the rope on occasion.

I caught the whiff of a dead slave hanging from a tree a couple miles back. You are not only losing valuable stock by hangings, you are having uprisings, slaves are running away, your crops are sometimes left in the fields too long for maximum profit, you suffer occasional fires, your animals are killed. Gentlemen, you know what your problems are; I do not need to enumerate your problems, I am here to introduce you to a method of solving them. In my bag here, I have a foolproof method for controlling your black slaves, I guarantee every one of you that, if installed correctly, will control the slaves for at least three hundred years. My method is simple. Any member of your family or your overseer can use it.

I have outlined a number of differences among the slaves, and I take these differences and make them bigger. I use distrust and envy for control purposes. These methods have worked on my modest plantation in the West Indies and it will work throughout the South. Take this simple little list of differences, and think about them. On top of my list is "Age", but it is there only because it starts with "A", the second is "Color" or shade, there is intelligence, size, sex, size of plantations, status on plantations, attitude of owners, whether the slaves live in the valley, on a hill, East, West, North, South, have fine hair, coarse hair, or is tall or short.

Now that you have a list of differences, I shall give you an outline of action, but before that, I shall assure you that distrust is stronger than trust, and envy is stronger than adulation, respect or admiration. The Black slave after receiving this introduction shall carry on and will become self-refueling and self-generating for hundreds of years, maybe thousands.

Don't forget you must pitch the old Black male vs. the young Black male, and the young Black male against the old Black male.

You must use the dark skin vs. the light skin slaves, and the light skin slaves vs. the dark skin slaves.

You must use the female vs. the male, and the male vs. the female. You must also have your white servants and overseers distrust all Blacks, but it is necessary that your slaves trust and depend on us. They must love, respect and trust only us. Gentlemen, these kits are your keys to control.

Use them. Have your wives and children use them, never miss an opportunity. If used intensely for one year, the slaves themselves will remain perpetually distrustful.

Thank you gentlemen,

Willie Lynch

Those of us who decided that we were going to invest all we had to try to stay in Harlem and make it work, made the decision because we believed that we had a right to be in business.

I also believed that I could serve the people of Harlem and the city of New York as well as any entrepreneur, and better than most because of the knowledge and understanding that comes from the particular experience I've had. This would include my quickly emerging (in my twenties) from the most prevalent class of work available to an African

American woman at that time, a maid—as an entrepreneur, with a shirt-laundering service for N.Y.U. students in Greenwich Village; having led a day care and advocacy movement for children and the poor; started and run three daycare centers and built a state-of-the-art, custom building to house one of them; and founded and led the Westside Community Alliance, Inc. which worked with people and agencies in all sectors of human life—legislation, education, politics, government, social service, science, media, commerce, finance, healthcare, law enforcement, religion, music & art, and serviced too many areas of need to go into here; and successfully owned and run a business that trained my three daughters, and several other people's children in business, service, dignity and ownership; and served the community in the process, during my seventeen years in Harlem as a businesswoman. I did not, and still do not believe anyone can question the acumen I have demonstrated, or the value of my presence in business.

Chapter Nine

Sojourner

During my residency in Harlem, my family and I often hosted people at our house on 138th Street. In my childhood home in Georgia, I was raised in the tradition of sharing, serving and hospitality. Upon settling in our brownstone home in Harlem we immediately began what would become a tradition of hosting friends, and dignitaries, just as my parents had hosted the visiting preachers who traveled in rotation to and from churches around the country in our church Association.

Often I would get a call from someone who had "visitors" and, that night, I would cook great southern meals of two or three different kinds of meats, fried fish, black eyed peas, collards and mustard greens, corn bread, green beans, okra, potato salad, cakes and pitchers of sweet iced tea and lemonade. One such night, we hosted the cast of a Broadway show.

Among the many guests we enjoyed hosting were luminaries of America's cultural, artistic, educational and political life. People including Angela Davis, Alice Walker, Jim Brown, James Earl Jones and his father, Historians John Henrik Clarke and Dr. Ben, attorney and activist Florence Kennedy, Gloria Steinem, artist Tom Feelings, Barbara Bundo, Phil Donohue and Princess Gloria von Thurn und Taxis from Bavaria, Germany spent evenings with us mingling and talking, singing songs around the piano and getting to know one another.

The NBA basketball team, the NY Knicks came once a year for three seasons for a special southern dinner and we all sat around and ate and talked in the backyard. We hosted Jesse Jackson and his mother during his campaign for the Presidency. Mrs. Jackson stayed several nights with us. And when Jesse's aunt passed we gave the repast at our house.

I hosted a party for Alex Haley and 300 people, many of whom he brought from Africa during his "Roots" project. Saim Kinte was among the few who stayed with us, while the others were in hotels. Saim met his cousin for the first time at our house, when Alex introduced him to his daughter, Anne Haley. The presence of the entourage, and the drumming that night enriched the whole street.

Authors, John Oliver Killins and Lofton Mitchell were guests. A talented young opera singer was one of the many students who stayed with us while studying at New York's fine arts schools. Sometimes, the gatherings became planning and rap sessions for making new inroads into creating meaningful solutions to fear, injustice, prejudice and abuse. New, international connections that supported African American-owned business were made. A UN ambassador from Africa who often had dinner with us hired the Cotton Club Band with my younger sister, Alice Ridley to play at the opening of his son's hotel in Morocco. It was a first trip to Africa for Alice, my youngest daughter Angela (who accompanied her) and the band.

I had held impromptu gatherings and black tie parties at my house. I was already running a de-facto B&B. With that, and the new government direction and dedication to bringing about Harlem's "New Renaissance", I decided to purchase another brownstone (between 124th and 125th Streets on 5th Avenue), and to open Harlem's First Guest House since the first Harlem Renaissance.

The second brownstone was just around the corner from Harlem Office Supply, which was located at 125th Street between 5th and 6th Avenues. It sat in the middle of a short block, butted right up against Marcus

Garvey Place, which runs along the North end of Marcus Garvey Park. It was an idyllic location; the building was essentially, "on the park".

I began the planning and renovation, and named it, "The Sojourner Guest House", after the great speaker, agitator, suffragist and abolitionist, Sojourner Truth. Several celebrities lent their support, including: Pulitzer Prize winning author, Alice Walker and her daughter, writer and actress Rebecca Walker; actors, Morgan Freeman; columnist and television host, Flo Anthony, Melba Moore, Bill Cosby, Whoopi Goldberg, Joie Lee, Freda Payne, John Beatty and several others. Gloria Steinem came to work on the project with us, along with friends and family of developer Mark Zuckerman; and Wilber Tatum, publisher of the Amsterdam News, Warner LeRoy of Tavern on the Green and Samuel Peabody of the Peabody Family.

Samuel brought in one of America's most renowned Architects, Peter Marino, and designer Mark Hampton to ensure that the Sojourner Guest House would be a showcase worthy of Harlem's history and the hopes we had for its future. We were sure that this would add attraction for tourism in New York and Harlem; as well as provide a great lift in terms of jobs and training, links to new and old businesses in the form of contracts for goods and services, and economic empowerment to residents in general.

We expected to complete The Sojourner Guest House by the summer of 1996. We spent our money locally at Harlem businesses in the renovation and all aspects of preparing to open the B&B.

We presented a "Harlem Savoy Dance Evening of Elegance", held September 30, 1995 at the National Black Theater on 5th Avenue as a benefit for the start up. Carol Jenkins, Anchorwoman at NBC News, hosted an appreciation reception. The committee members were Flo Anthony, Mark Hampton, Peter Marion, H. Carl McCall, Samuel Peabody, Marlene Schiff, Barbara Smith, Gloria Steinem and myself.

As part of the evening's events, a special salute was given to Congressman Charles Rangel, the Honorable Percy E. Sutton, the Honorable Andrew

Cuomo, Ms. Hilda Stokely, Ms. LaChonne Oliver, Ms. Elizabeth F. Harris and Attorney Cora Walker.

In addition, public thanks were given to some people who helped to garner the level of support we had, including: Councilwoman C. Virginia Fields, Borough President Ruth Messinger, Councilman Adam Clayton Powell IV, Senator David Paterson, Assemblyman Keith Wright, Iris Berner, Delethia Marvin, Hubert Collins, Angela Hughes, Alice Ridley, Patrice Quinn, Yvonne Rose, John Beatty, Bobby Robinson, Pat Swann, and Attorney Coral T. Walker, Gloria Dulan Wilson, Clarence Hughes, Jean Berry, Grace Richmond, Bill Pitman, Mel & Mary Williams, Mary Cunningham, Mildred Dent, Alma Scott, Luther Seabrook, Joan Hamilton and Lena Meyers.

The support these people had given now and over the years would have served, under what should have been normal circumstances, to help put a floor on an economic base in Harlem. At the time, I believed we were all helping to secure our businesses in Harlem; now I believe getting the help and attention we did made us more vulnerable. It seems we might have been more "successful", if we had aspired to be "servants and workers", but because we worked at creating *ownership* for people of color, there was difficulty.

Proposal to the UMEZ:

With the planning underway, and stellar support for the project, we were ready to approach the EZ. I was aware that our proposal would need to be well done, and by a professional, so I hired a consultant who was recommended to me by one of our Harlem political leaders. The consultant and I worked together; I gave him my plan, and he wrote the proposal. And I presented the proposal to the UMEZ.

The result: The paid consultant who wrote my proposal was hired at UMEZ, in charge of evaluating the proposals of other businesses; my proposal was denied, and I soon learned through the EZ's newsletter that my new next door neighbor, Jane Alex Mendelson would be opening a B & B at 2005 5th Avenue, right next door to the proposed home of The Sojourner Guest House, at 2007 5th Avenue.

I went to visit my new European American neighbor. I asked her about the project, and if I could see her proposal. She said she didn't have one; that shortly after she had purchased her 1878 brownstone building the EZ had called her and asked if she would be willing to open a guest house there. She told them she knew "nothing" about opening or running a guest house, and they responded saying that they "already had a proposal", that they "were going to fund it", and they wanted her to do it. She said they "convinced" her, and so she was gifted an investment of $50,000 (not to be repaid) from BRISC—the EZ's agency evaluating proposals for funding. And she was given a UMEZ Loan for $379,000 to complete and open "The Urban Gem Guest House", Harlem's first B & B since our renaissance.

Chapter Ten

Copeland's

The black business owners who were the most successful seemed to be under attack. In 1997 Mr. Calvin Copeland, at the age of 82, was forced to close his 226-seat restaurant on 125th Street. Copeland's Restaurants had survived the riots in Harlem, but could not survive the renewal. He owned two restaurants in Harlem, one on 145th Street on the Westside and Copeland's Country Kitchen on 125th Street. Both were doing well. He had just borrowed and spent 1.3 million dollars in improvements to the 125th Street restaurant, the closure of which was sparked by the announcement of the funding of the EZ in Harlem. The landlord of the building where Mr. Copeland built his business was McDonald's Corporation. Soon after the 1.3 million dollar restoration and announcement of the EZ, McDonald's Corp. raised his rent considerably, to $22,000 a month.

Mr. Copeland tried unsuccessfully to either negotiate a reduction in rent or make a deal that would allow him to partner with someone. McDonald's Corporation refused all proposals from Mr. Copeland, who lost his business and had to fire 60 workers—some trainees; most, Harlem and Bronx residents. McDonald's Corporation, for years, had rented their property to Mr. Copeland and others, and built their stores elsewhere. There was a McDonald's store down the street. At that time, Laura Vega was spokeswoman for McDonald's Corporation and revealed no information on what the 1.3 million dollar-improved property would be used for after the eviction of Copeland's Restaurant. Mr. Copeland received no help from the EZ, in either keeping his business, relocating, or repaying his loan, for which he had put up his house and his other business as collateral. W.I.S.E. was able to help him separate the two businesses, so he would not lose both at once. He lost his second business in 2007.

Normally, the closing of this seemingly forward moving business would become a setback for our political leaders to receive any financial support for the development of Harlem. How could our leaders justify Mr. Copeland's spending 1.3 million dollars and then being evicted as part of an Empowerment Zone effort? They did not seem worried about the friction between the corporate community and the local business community at all. Nor did they seem to notice or care that the stated intention of the EZ was clearly being ignored by its leadership.

At a certain point during this whole process, I actually followed some of our Harlem leadership one evening to a downtown hotel, where they met with men from the City. I was seeing first-hand who was really in control of Harlem's politics and economy.

National retailers continued to scout Harlem and the Bronx for expansion opportunities. The local business owners knew that we were not just dealing with local leaders, we were also up against corporate, state and national entities.

Chapter Eleven

I'm Just Saying...

At first, many of the male business owners took issue with the name of our organization. W.I.S.E. held a meeting to which we invited all business owners in Harlem who wished to be represented and involved in the Empowerment Zone, and the men didn't show up. We continued to work on their behalf and our own; and eventually, it was clear that since we were all being pushed out, it would be wiser to recognize that we all needed to work together.

Shange Sikhulu, a Harlem resident since 1964, was the owner of the **Record Shack**, established in 1975. Shange Sikhulu was doing everything he could for all African and African American businesses to be included in the EZ plan. The then 25-year-old record store on 125th Street, specialized in Caribbean, African Blues and Motown music—"ethnic" music very important to our culture. He discussed with the leaders of Harlem his concern that UMEZ was bringing in the Harlem USA complex (a mall) and not including the Record Shack. His concerns were ignored. Shange Sikhula held on to his business until 2010, never receiving a dime from the EZ, just being pushed out.

...It Looks Like Ethnic Cleansing:

The **Gadabout Restaurant** on 5th Avenue was owned by Ms. Sam, who was interested in raising her children and other children in Harlem to be business owners, was one of the first to have her rent increased by thousands of dollars. She was soon put out of business.

Mr. Joseph Wells and Mrs. Ann Wells were the owners of **Wells Chicken and Waffles** at 243 Adam Clayton Powell Boulevard, first opened in 1938. It was noted in the NY Times that the restaurant was scheduled to close and move in 1984. The Wells' tried to get help from our leaders after having kept it open for years. The help was promised but it never came.

It is well known that some of the most successful businesses in Harlem traditionally have been restaurants and clubs. We consistently had thousands of visitors to Harlem, even through the years of decay. Wells' food was famous. This long-standing, still vibrant business was a perfect business to receive support from the EZ. Even when Mrs. Wells chose to follow the instructions given to her by Congressman Rangel's office to cancel her membership in W.I.S.E., the Empowerment Zone did not help her. Restaurants are still needed and profitable in "new" Harlem. Soon after Wells' Restaurant closed, another restaurant, not African American owned, was given the EZ funding.

Bill's Hardware store, after operating successfully for many years, was forced to close. W.I.S.E. petitioned constantly to the EZ to simply give Bill's Hardware the contract to supply just the nails to any one of the new building projects in Harlem, and watch what he could do to sustain and grow his longtime business, even without any loans or tax cuts or any of what he might have expected from a sincere empowerment program.

Georgia's Donut Shop was a favorite spot that had a line around the block two times daily, in the mornings and afternoons, for their unrivaled fresh, hot donuts and pies. They existed long before anyone ever heard of Krispy Kreme—which produces hot donuts, but not nearly of the same nutritional quality or taste—was brought in to replace them.

The **National Black Theater**, which consistently drew large audiences and trained and fostered our great talent, like many of our other true cultural centers, was under much pressure to close, but some young African American men from Brooklyn stepped up and saved it.

The **125th Street Mart**, where independent merchants were able to set up shop and alleviate the crowding of street vending, closed.

Chapter Twelve

The Strategic Planning Process

The following is taken from materials we generated on the planning committee. This is the information given to us by the EZ and which we then presented to the people of the community.

Over 1,100 people came together to provide the "bottom up" participation, which was an integral component of the strategic planning process for the Harlem EZ. They came together for community meetings and in sixteen working groups that focused on specific issues or problems critical to the process.

Individuals on the working groups represented residents, Community Board members, and practitioners in specific fields, such as: school superintendents, housing developers, police officers, hospital administrators, clergy, business people, and service providers. The community working groups were charged with crafting vision statements related to their areas of expertise and for providing input into the strategic planning process. The working groups met frequently throughout the planning process to formulate a vision for their particular needs. The working groups' vision statements, which reflected their efforts to provide a realistic outlook of what the Harlem EZ could become, provided the basis for further analysis by technicians working with the community to formulate the Strategic Plan.

In many cases the working groups brought together people and institutions providing the same services to the same populations who had never before sat at the same table to share information. For example, Harlem's six hospitals came together for the first time to discuss the best ways to provide health care services to the community.

When all the working groups met to integrate their visions and their strategies, it became apparent that they could improve the services across the board by sharing resources and coordinating efforts. A wide range of service providers could begin to track a child right from prenatal care, through day care, through grade school, and up until college or other alternative preparation for the job market.

The African proverb, "It takes a village to raise a child" best describes our approach as a community. This philosophy explains the objectives in our Strategic Plan to coordinate activities and programs related to children and to youth.

Social services play a key role in assuring that people are able to take advantage of economic opportunities. Unless there is adequate childcare and without healthcare, they are not able to participate in the labor force.

Social services in the EZ community were not only inadequate, they were also fragmented and uncoordinated. The objectives set forth in the Strategic Plan were directed at increasing funding for a wide range of support services, such as day care and primary health care. They were also directed at reinventing the way in which services were delivered by consolidating them at the neighborhood level in family-based invest-ment centers.

The foundation of the strategic plan rested on an integrated set of visions articulated by the working groups. Creating a vision was a precursor to the development of strategies and programs. A participant at the first meeting said it well: "I can't build this house until I know how I want it to look."

Each of the working groups shaped a strategic vision. Their visions encompassed suggestions made at a "youth speak-out", and during an intensive ten-week grassroots planning process in Harlem. Planning efforts in the South Bronx were rooted in a program initiative called, "New Directions from the Bronx," culminating with a series of town hall meetings. Both communities engaged in a process to define their "bottom-up" community planning vision.

The overall implementation strategy had five interrelated parts: Strategic Plan, Community Participation, Governance, Evaluation, and Adjustment.

Strategic Plan:

The Empowerment Strategic Plan is to be the contract for implementation. Participation of the local development corporation and zone residents will be requirements for any changes and adjustments to the plan.

Governance:

A local/city/state public benefit corporation (the "Corporation") was created to help implement the strategic plan described within this application. The Corporation is a subsidiary of the New York State Urban Development Corporation and was governed by a Board of Directors. The Board was composed of representatives from Harlem, the South Bronx, the City of New York, and the State of New York. The Corporation was chartered for the life of the zone with members of the board appointed for equal terms.

The Corporation was required by contract with HUD to work within the framework of the EZ Strategic Plan developed by (and to be modified in accordance with) the EZ Community. Working in close partnership with the local development corporations (LDCs), one representing the communities of Harlem (designated by the Congressional Representative for the 15th District), the corporation serves as the fulcrum for city, state and federal aid and would:

1) coordinate city and state funding agencies
2) expedite the funding of EZ contracts

3) ensure compliance of city and state agencies with the strategic plan

4) coordinate the process of evaluating and modifying the strategic plan with respect to the disbursement of city and state funding.

However, it was not intended that the Corporation undertake any day-to-day administrative activities such as the actual custody, management or disbursement of funds or the entry into contracts with service providers on any particular project. Administration of the contracts developed by the LDCs would be done by the funding agencies and through the local development corporations. All funds were to be approved and disbursed through the local development corporation.

Two local development corporations (LDCs) were to be responsible for implementing the EZ Strategic Plan. One LDC would represent the Bronx EZ Community and the other, the Harlem EZ community. In Harlem, the Congressional Representative of the 15th District designated an LDC. The major functions of the LDCs would be the administration and implementation of the plan. Other functions included direction, the execution of contracts with service providers, negotiating contracts, and authorizing and dispensing checks.

We were told that the LDCs would account for all expenditures of EZ funds. At the request of the LDC, the Public Benefit Corporation would direct federal, state, and city funds earmarked for the EZ to the state and/or city comptroller, who would administer the funds for the LDC and deposit them in an EZ-based bank.

- The LDC would have sole authority to approve disbursement of EZ funds.

- The LDC would not spend funds for purposes other than those compatible with the goals outlined in the EZ Strategic Plan.

- The LDC would have sole authority to approve contracts utilizing funds earmarked for the EZ.

- Contracts providing government-funded services to the EZ would be administered by relevant state and city agencies.

- EZ programs directly funded by private and/or federal sources would be administered by the LDC.

The LDC would make available to the public the type and cost of services provided by the government in the EZ, such as housing and business ownership data, business and employment data, as well as current information on government grants and contracts.

The development vision had at its center the family and child, extending from early childhood and youth and from adulthood to seniors. It was a preventive vision that provided a full range of services within redesigned systems. It was supposedly a vision that was non-punitive and non-stigmatizing. It was to be one of speedy, effective and efficient programming and delivery of human services to EZ residents through advanced communications networks, utilizing modern information technologies.

Human Development:

The human development vision spoke to independence and self-sufficiency. There was to be an investment strategy that would enable residents to have full participation in the process. Residents were to be full partners in the planning, design, and implementation of programs that impacted their lives. It was to be a vision defined by mutual respect and responsibility. It was intergenerational and grounded in the cultures, values, and ethics of the EZ community. Collaborative efforts, coordinated actions and mutual responsibility with new partners were to be the center of human development.

Physical Development:

Physical development was integrated with environmental factors of design, planning, and development of residential, commercial, industrial and transportation projects. Housing was to be developed without displacement. Home ownership opportunities were to be available for all income levels. The transportation network would be further developed to link the EZ with the metropolitan and regional economies. The EZ community was to benefit from activities that would accrue from the physical development of the EZ. The infrastructure was to be linked to the world through advanced communications and new systems of information technology that would be part of the information superhighway. Public safety benefits would accrue both from economic opportunities and the physical redevelopment.

EZ residents made clear their desire for the opportunity to improve their lives through greater access to affordable higher education and effective job training, through quality jobs that offer challenging work and more benefits and health care, as well as a fair chance for promotion. They wished to see improvements in the safety and maintenance of their current housing and the opportunity to own their housing. And it had been proven, and acknowledged that none of this is possible unless a level of economic security could be obtained that would allow them to afford the initial "down payment".

The residents wanted to see more affordable and safe day care centers. The problem of drug sales, drug abuse, and related street crimes were serious problems reported by residents. Polls were taken to determine what the residents thought the best available solutions to these and other problems would be. The solutions were broad-based and comprehensive. Respondents wanted an increase in the number of jobs (76%); better job training (66%); drug prevention programs for the young (63%); and better access to college (62%).

Finding a good job and moving up to a better job were clearly important to residents, personally and as a critical component of improving the quality of life in the community. Of the 73% who responded to an open-ended question, employed and unemployed residents suggested that the government offered affordable, accessible job training (24%); did more to create new jobs (18%); provided regular listing of available jobs (13%); and made higher education affordable and accessible (12%).

When asked to evaluate ten specific projects proposed for the community, there was strong support for all of the projects. When asked to choose the one or two they would most like developed, a center for career training in information technology (37%) and new housing development (36%) were the most popular programs followed by recreational and cultural facilities for teenagers (26%); day care centers for working parents (19%); a new business and commercial center for creating jobs (17%) and a center for training in the constructions trades (16%).

When asked to suggest additional projects, one third of those interviewed responded. Projects related to social and health services (33%); safety/anti-crime programs (12%); community centers (12%) and education programs (11%) were the most frequently mentioned.

Donald Cogsville, President and CEO of the Harlem Urban Development Corp., the government entity in charge of writing the proposal for funding of the EZ, stated in a letter to James P. Murphy, the Executive Vice President of Fleet Financial Group, that "underlying the success of the Empowerment Zone was the opportunity for every able resident to be employed." Unemployment of African Americans who lived in the zone had reached a level of over 16%. Cogsville wrote that "without services, thousands of residents would not be helped in the zone". He acknowledged long suffering in efforts to improve conditions for people in the Harlem and Bronx communities and he stated that it was essential that we were provided employment, training, and childcare in the zone. He also made reference to the popularity of Harlem, being known as the capital of African America. Its most important asset, he said, was the "spirit of its people." Thousands of photos were taken and submitted. And he made it a point to state that the application was prepared with full participation of the entire community, "with no segment omitted".

Chapter Thirteen

Funding and Support

Fleet Bank was introduced as one of the banks that were committing to credit initiatives with the collateral from the federal dollars. Fleet was to make loans to our small African American-owned businesses, home mortgages and more economic revitalization initiatives providing capital and credit, community initiatives, capital that would be focused on education efforts, and diversity. Executive Vice President James P. Murphy said that Fleet would commit $7.5 million in loans, including micro loans for businesses. Fleet was establishing a CDC with an initial capitalization of $15 million and $25 million financing in affordable housing. There was not an amount stated for the community initiatives, which were designated for credit education, charitable giving, college scholarships, and employment opportunities for minority students living in the zone.

A June 27, 1994 letter from the office of the Mayor to Secretary Henry G. Cisneros stated that the leadership had innovative strategies to create real jobs in the zone area, improve social services and health care delivery that would allow zone residents to take full advantage of those jobs to preserve safer, cleaner neighborhoods where families and businesses would continue to move in and stay. The mayor stated that he viewed the Empowerment Zone program as a renewed investment to revitalize those urban communities.

City of New York:

In a climate of severe fiscal constraints and shrinking resources, the Mayor of the City of New York made a commitment to invest $100 million in the revitalization of the zone and was in agreement with the community's priorities as set forth in the Strategic Plan. The city would spend an estimated $1.5 billion in capital projects in the EZ over ten years. In addition, the city would participate with the community in reinventing the way government delivered services in the EZ, and in reviewing requests for relief or elimination of regulatory barriers. A representative of the Mayor's office served as part of the EZ coordinating team since the initial days of the strategic planning process and was one of two full-time people assigned to the EZ from the Office of the Mayor. All major city agencies were involved in the planning process, as were the director of the city's Office of Management and Budget and the Deputy Mayor for Finance and Economic Development.

State of New York:

The Governor of the State of New York made a commitment to invest $100 million in the revitalization of the EZ and was in agreement with the community's priorities as set forth in the Strategic Plan. In addition, the state was to participate with the community in reinventing the way government delivered services in the EZ and in reviewing requests for relief or elimination of regulatory barriers. A representative of the Governor's office served as part of the EZ coordination team since the initial days of the strategic process and was on full-time assignment to the EZ. All major state agencies had been involved in the planning process as had the director of the state's Budget Office and the Chair, President and CEO of Urban Development Corporation, the State's economic development arm.

Private Support:

Representatives of private sector companies and non-profit entities located in the EZ and in other parts of New York City provided ongoing technical and staff assistance to the EZ coordination team and served on the various issue-based working groups. A broad range of private sector companies and non-profit entities made commitments to support the implementation of the plan by providing financial assistance and technical expertise to the community. The economic development strategies in the plan were developed under the leadership of the chambers of commerce, business alliances, and board of realtors within the EZ. Discussions were underway with representatives from regional and private sector under the aegis of the New York City Partnership, the primary business organization in the city, to increase commitments and to join with the local leadership in implementing the Strategic Plan.

Institutional Support:

Harlem Hospital Center, Mt. Sinai Medical Center, North General Hospital, Presbyterian Hospital, and St. Luke's/Roosevelt Hospital Center collectively agreed to participate in a consortium of EZ health care providers and to engage in joint planning efforts to redress primary care and other health care needs. We understood that the two teaching hospitals, Mount Sinai and Columbia Presbyterian, were committing resources to further expand biotechnology activities in the Harlem community. Columbia University, the City University of New York (CUNY), City College of the City University of New York, the four-year CUNY College located in Harlem, and Hostos Community College were committed to bringing resources to the EZ to improve the educational opportunities for Zone residents. Columbia, CUNY, and City College provided technical expertise to the EZ coordinating committee throughout the strategic planning process.

The Federal Government:

The $100 million in SSBG funds that the community was to receive, if designated as an Empowerment Zone, would be used to implement the Strategic Plan as follows:

- 20% for job and work force development
- 20% for housing and neighborhood
- 3% for infrastructure

- 22% for children and youth
- 12% for health and substance abuse
- 6% for services
- 17% for administration

We, the people of these communities laid the groundwork to ensure the availability and high quality of basic support services in the EZ. If the plan had been inclusive, Harlem would be a meaningful and beautiful place for the people who lived there then. In order to contemplate the question of whether what occurred was in fact 'ethnic cleansing", take a look around Harlem today and ask yourself: Who were to be the beneficiaries of all this?

Chapter Fourteen

"Hold This Whip"

When my family and I moved to Harlem, I very consciously decided to work to create a model for economic inclusion of African American owned businesses in Harlem. If there was to be a successful model created, it could work in all African American and/ or poor communities. The issues are the same: home ownership, business ownership, real education from early childhood through college, job training and jobs, social and economic empowerment, and finally local political empowerment. The "leadership" of Harlem and the city officials were planning a different model and I'm just saying... *it looks like Ethnic Cleansing.*

The following Harlem businesses existed when I was in business on 125th Street:

ABC Service Center
Afrika Market Place
Afrika House
Akbar's Antiques 145th Street
Akbar's Antiques 125th Street
All Souls Episcopal Church
Alpha Construction
Apollo Theatre
Baobab Tree, Inc.
Bazaar Beauty Supply Barn
Benjamin Medical Center
Benta's Funeral Home, Inc.
Better Crust Bakery
Big Red Newspaper
Billy's Night Club
Black Fashion Museum, The
Brown Sugar Models, Inc.
Carol P. Bellamy Agency, Ins.
Cellar Restaurant, The
Club Key Limousine
Chemical Bank (All Branches)
Citibank B'way & 11th Street
Citibank Amsterdam & 124th St.
Citibank 1st Ave and 116th St.
Citibank B'way & 171st Street
Citibank B'way & 196th Street
Copland's Restaurant
Davis Hall (Aaron At CCNY)
Dee's Cards n' Wedding Service
Development Outreach
E and G Antiques
FAS Productions
Fantasy Lounge
Four Steps Boutique, The
Fragrance Lab, Inc., The
Georgette's Unisex Beauty Salon
Global Business Institute
Good News Newsstand 149th St.

Good News Newsstand 145th Street
Gumbs & Thomas, Publishers
Greenidge-Joiner Mortgage Brokers
H&L Contractor's Plus
Hair in Motion, Inc.
Hair Weaving By Evelyn
Harlem Athletic Association
Harlem Agency, (Insurance)
Harlem Copy Center
Harlem Graphic Arts Center
Harlem Hospital
Harlem YMCA
Harlem, Your Way! Tours UNL
Henry W. Payne, Inc. Funeral Directors
Hoover Brothers Meat Market
I Am Your Florist
J&L Parking, Inc. 125th St. Municipal
J&L Parking, Inc. 129th Street
J&L Parking and Hand Car Wash
J&L Parking Polo Ground Site
Jamaican Hot Pot Restaurant
Jewel's Lounge
J.R. Hansborough Jr. Rec. Ctr. Bath House
Lenny's Video Box
Leisure Lovers
Majester's Fish & Chips
M. Marshall Blake Funeral Home
Malcolm-King Harlem College Ext.
Mary's Newsstand 135th St.
Medina Youth Center
Michael Kennedy Lloyd, Esq.
Charles House of Greetings
Mid-Manhattan NAACP
Mt. Olivet Baptist Church
National Black Theatre
Nat's Bar
North General Hospital Gift Shop
Northern Lights Restaurant

Operation Helping Hand
Our Children's Development Inst.
Our Family Deli & Sweet Shop
Oz Liquor Co. Buy Rite
Paragon Cable
Powder Puff By Marion
Rice High School
Riverside Church
Ron Spence Assoc. Conference Plan
Rucker Professionals, Inc.
St. Martin's Episcopal Church
St. Phillips Episcopal Church
Showman's Cafe
Singleton's BBQ
South Carolina Heating Fuel, Inc.
Star's Record & Video

Strivers row Photo 139th St.
Sugar Hill Doll Co.
Sylvia's Restaurant
Turning Heads Beauty & Barber
22 West Restaurant
Twilight, Night Life Magazine
Uptown Chamber of Commerce
Uptown Tennis & Fitness Center
Urban Business Initiative, Inc.
Vantage Marketing Services
WJE Travel
Wilson Bakery & Restaurant
WBLS/WLIB
Yolandia's Show Room
Young Newsstand 138th St. & 7th
Yvon-Maye Carefree Travel

Three businesses that remain include: **Sylvia's Restaurant**, the **Cotton Club** and **Abyssinian Church**. If there are any others, I haven't been able to reach them by phone…so I am doubtful of their survival.

African Americans were set up in business to manage the closings of the legitimate African American-owned business. See who owns these so-called African American businesses now, and follow the trail of which in the leadership, you can track to the new ownership.

I took in a young guy whom I watched being mentally abused by his boss. I trained him, and made him a manager in my business. Later, the EZ set him up in his own copy service business as my competitor. He eventually opened a small chain of stores. I am told that now, since the gentrification of Harlem is almost complete, he has suffered, losing each of them but one, which is also threatened with closure. The people who used him for their own political, financial, and social gain will not be there for him.

Generally, the holders of the "whip" will be the officers of a church, politicians, or wanna-be politicians, or just anyone suffering from the "Willie Lynch Syndrome". In Harlem, it was all of the above.

Chapter Fifteen

"Now, Beat Your Mama!"

Our political leaders explained to us that in order to help achieve EZ goals, they sought to foster partnerships between the large corporations they were bringing in and community residents, businesspersons, financial institutions, service providers, neighborhood associations, and state and local governments.

A meeting was held at Congressman Charles Rangel's office with H.O.S. and Staples, the national copying, printing, and office supply store, with whom I would soon be competing unless it were made possible for us to co-exist. There were representatives from all of the Harlem political offices and the noted African American church, Abyssinian Baptist Church.

Today I think of the people in that meeting and I wonder if they ever thought of the positive difference they could have made in their own lives and in the lives of other Harlem families. They could have helped create real economic empowerment. We were all aware that without economic empowerment, we will never have social or political freedom.

We were all getting older. We could have been spending our time securing an economic base for the children of Harlem. There were plenty of us who at that time believed in our representatives... believed that they were interested in us and in the diversity....and we tried to help them work with us.

I did then, and still do have, the highest respect for the Honorable Percy Sutton. I gave fund raising events for whomever he recommended. I made time and financial contributions. I organized childcare services, social events, African American owned businesses, and youth employment. I believe Mr. Sutton had an understanding of what it is really possible to do. He was aware of the every day heroics of African Americans and our long and necessary tradition of working for radical change. He was not confused by his success. He was never under the spell of "middle-class" or "bourgeois" notions that there was only "so much" one person could do, and so he was not the type to just try and "get his slice of the pie". He was a person of vision; and he had the energy and strength to believe in vision, and invest in it.

In earlier years, I had organized the housing squatters movements and the closing of welfare hotels. When my middle daughter was fifteen, I bought the "Miss America Pageant" franchise for the Greater New York area and helped change the face of Miss America after 53 years. Percy applauded my work always, and never considered that I might be getting "too big for my britches" or responded as if I were stepping "out of my place". He had been a worker, as I, and many others had been, in a longtime movement for the rights of African Americans as citizens of this country; and he would not be satisfied until his work was done.

And now our movement was about to become blessed in Harlem. We were the first to participate in a federal project called the "Empowerment Zone". WOW! We joined committees and we worked. I was happy to be listed as a committee person. I worked on committees with Latinos, Asians, and other ethnicities, and represented them all as small business owners and residents of Harlem.

Reginald and Catherine James of **NuApple-Harlem USA** created a map of the African American owned businesses in the Empowerment Zone. The map represented us as the "core of the apple". The map featured words some Harlem residents used to describe their hometown: "creative", "beautiful", "crazy energy", "mesmerizing". At that time Harlem was home to thousands of African Americans whose common roots are their African ancestry. The community reflected a rich history and culture and was recognized over the world as The Black Mecca. Harlem also became famous for its entertainment spots, nightclubs, restaurants, churches, shops, and architecture. Harlem could be considered home to African Americans across the country.

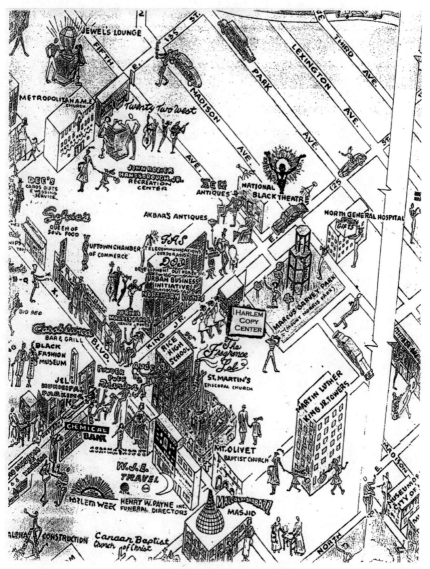

This is a portion of the NuApple-Harlem USA map that includes Harlem Copy Center / Harlem Office Supply, Inc.

African American business owners were happily welcoming The Empowerment Zone, as it was portrayed by our congressman and others. We were herded into meeting halls to hear of the wonderful things that were to happen in Harlem. And then we watched our African American leaders give support and loans to made-up 'Harlem' businesses, and to corporations and entities like Staples, Foot Locker, Disney and TriBeca Films—as they carried out the plan, which, I'm just saying… *it looks like Ethnic Cleansing.*

Chapter Sixteen

Staples

About three weeks after the meeting at Congressman Rangel's office with Staples and the representatives from Abyssinian Church, I attended a party for the retirement of the founder of Carver Bank. There I met a deacon from Abyssinian. After having consumed quite a bit of alcohol, he walked over to me and decided to tell me how stupid I was.

Because of its past leader, Adam Clayton Powell, Jr., I would say most Harlemites would have expected that anyone who came in to replace him at Abyssinian would care for the whole community, not just his "class" group. We trusted church leadership. That evening, this gentleman was eager to let me in on a little secret. He said to me: "We are going to get rid of you, we are working on a deal with Staples." He explained that he and his church board were going to put me out of business; and that I, being a woman, could not run an office supply company. They were bringing in Staples and Staples was going to hire all of its workers from his church. He explained with particular glee that they had known that I would give up my plan and information if the meeting was held at "Charlie's" office. There was a time when I was quite fond of the congressman, and endearingly called him "Charlie". I considered him a friend and colleague, as he had worked very hard and well for our community. After all, he had initiated the Empowerment Zone legislation. I never perceived a problem with any of the Harlem leadership until the actual entrance of the Empowerment Zone.

On that last point, the deacon was right. I had given them my information. I had not recognized them as the "blacks" with the "master's whip." I did not want to believe that African Americans would be so selfish as to economically, socially, and spiritually damage a person who, with her total existence, had served the community. Did our leaders feel nothing as they used poor adults and children to get 300 million city, state and federal dollars? Our leaders knew that the children they spoke about in their letters to the Mayor and the federal government would not be helped in Harlem. They knew that the parents of these children would not own businesses; and, because of their "class" most likely would not get jobs in the new Empowerment Zone either.

Staples, with the help of the community leaders and Abyssinian Church, had decided that they wanted to come to Harlem. Moreover, they wanted to move into the storefront where Harlem Office Supply, Inc. was located, in a row of storefronts just beside the Harlem State Office Building on 125th Street. My rent was suddenly raised from $4,000, to $21,000 per month (by the City, who owned the structure), as we remained under capitalized. During the entire time we were in business in Harlem, we never received $10 from the Empowerment Zone.

In the 21st century, discrimination in Harlem would no longer be confined to race or sex, but religious preference and class would also be included. Economic isolation would become more acute.

The Empowerment Zone's material stated, in its "Introduction", that the mission and responsibility of the zone was to *change the economic, social and physical conditions* of persons, households, and neighborhoods in *poverty*, and to improve the overall quality of life of the existing residents. The theme throughout the application was one of economic empowerment and self-sufficiency. It was to develop strategies to lessen dependency and to improve economic mobility for families and individuals who lived and worked in the area.

It was also stated that three decades ago there had been a national focus to reduce poverty; and was acknowledged that massive intervention was needed to halt the growth of two *separate* and *unequal* societies, based on race and income. It was believed that because of race and income, the attention of the nation had gone to other matters.

The utilization of financial institutions located within the EZ would take priority to non-EZ financial institutions. Local administrative entities would be responsible for the implementation of the plan. The Harlem Local Development Corporation (HLDC) would direct the execution of contracts with service providers, negotiate the contracts, as well as develop programs/projects that would meet the strategic plan. This would mean bringing each Harlem small business to the table, evaluating the business with the committee and the business owner, determining what it would take to put that business in a position to grow and become self-sustaining; and helping to create the partnerships between the local businesses and outside corporations.

Harlem leadership announced how the bottom-up planning process would occur. They directed the community boards that they controlled to assign representatives to the EZ working groups. Because we had representatives from community-based organizations, elected officials, business owners, churches, professional associations and other local institutions, and non-affiliated residents as part of the team, we believed we had representation.

Chapter Seventeen

Clinton Comes To Harlem

I never got the chance to go to Washington to speak with the President about lifting the economic embargo against African American women in Harlem. But in 2000, I heard that President Bill Clinton was coming to Harlem with his new post-white house offices, so I prepared a welcome. As owner of Harlem Office Supply, Inc., located one block east of President Clinton's new office, I decided that a cake would be the perfect touch. At home in Georgia, whenever new neighbors moved into our community, we'd bake a cake and all the residents would gather to welcome them.

So I sent a letter to President Clinton on behalf of the African American owned businesses in Harlem who wanted to be included, to welcome him to Harlem. I asked if we could welcome him with a cake to allow the southern tradition of "if you are coming to the community to live with the people, we break bread together". A letter came back to us approving. The theme was "We Knew You Were Coming, So We Baked a Cake". I invited small businesses in Harlem of all ethnic groups. We, along with all our staffs, presented a cake to President Clinton inside the Harlem State Office Building, and after the ceremony the staff served some 2500 people with more cakes, from tables set up all around the square outside.

Egypt Lawson of Egypt Group (graphic design services), created a computerized cake design. We presented the plan to Wimp's Southern Style Bakery, just four doors down from President Clinton's office. Harlem

Office Supply, Inc. and Wimp's Bakery were sponsors for the cake-cutting presentation. Other participating businesses included: Mahmut Mauruk of H & M Gallery of Harlem (art and frame store), Carolyn Banks of Manhattan Paint Fair, Inc. (paint and hardware store), Doreen Barrett of Ethnic Elegance Salon (beauty and barber services), Bola of BOLA International Boutique (African fabrics and fashions), Eddie Ruiz of Dolphin Fitness Club of Harlem (fitness and nutrition), Delethia Marvin of Delethia's Catering Just For You (pasta, exotic salads and "din din" baskets), Nassen & Inrahim of 1938 Madison Avenue Deli (delicatessen and grocery store), Reggie Oliver of Teller New York Metro (business consulting), Henry Calderon of East Harlem Chamber of Commerce, Charles Gabriel of Charles' Southern Style Kitchen (southern food restaurant and catering), Yvonne and Tony Rose of Amber Books (self-help books for African Americans), Moctar Yata of Djema Imports (African fabrics, fashions & accessories), Pat Stevenson of Harlem News Group ("good news"), Dr. Barbara Ann Teer of The National Black Theatre (theatrical productions), Mr. & Mrs. John Mc Rae of McRae's Furniture, Inc. (new and used furniture) and Jim Elliott of Long Life Vitamins (vitamins and diet supplements).

On July 30th Winzle and Donna Wimp put the final touches on the beautiful cake, complete with various delectable fillers—strawberry, pineapple, lemon, chocolate and butter cream. Wimp's, which had been a mainstay in Harlem since 1979, was known for its world famous banana pudding, delicious apple & peach cobblers and sweet potato pie.

According to Winzle Wimp, who had acquired the bakery twenty-two years before, from his mother, "My wife Donna and I along with five staff members have been working on the cake for three days. I feel very special and honored to participate in this project. I know that President Clinton has a sweet tooth and I hope that once he tastes the cake he'll visit our store personally".

Later that day during a special reception at Sylvia's Restaurant, President Clinton stated, "the cake was a wonderful surprise. I cut it and tasted it—and it was delicious".

The day was filled with wonderful events, beginning with a VIP party, which was attended by a melting pot of prominent community leaders, business owners, celebrities and clergy. Reverend Dr. Wyatt T. Walker was pleased that former President Bill Clinton had chosen a Harlem address for his new office. "I think it's terrific for the morale of the people for a former President to have headquarters in Harlem, but more especially since it happens to be President Bill Clinton"—who at that time was the most inclusive President in the history of the Republic.

At the official ceremony, nearly 10,000 people greeted former President Bill Clinton with thunderous applause when he stepped on stage in front of the Adam Clayton Powell Jr. State Office Building on West 125th Street. Terry C. Lane, the President and CEO of the Upper Manhattan Empowerment Zone at the time, acknowledged and thanked the special guests and program sponsors and welcomed the enthusiastic spectators. Mistress of Ceremonies Cicely Tyson proclaimed, "This is a great day in Harlem!".

Congressman Charles Rangel, who was thanked personally by President Clinton for following up on his request to help him find office space in Harlem, spoke about the former President's move. He commented, "When Bill Clinton was elected President, we knew he was on our side. If we had our way, he would be re-elected". Rangel said that President Clinton's having given birth to the Empowerment Zone legislation brought attention to the underdeveloped areas that had not shared in the great prosperity of the 1990's; and he emphasized that Harlem is the flagship of the Empowerment Zone around the United States. He concluded, "We don't just get a former President, we get someone who understands what it takes. It doesn't surprise us that our President has come home to support us".

As President Clinton cut the cake, Congressman Rangel made sure to block me from the vicinity, and never acknowledged that I had organized that cake presentation.

Left to right: Terry Lane (UMEZ), Dorothy Pitman Hughes, Congressman Charles Rangel, President Clinton and Winzle Wimp.

Greetings were also extended by Honorable David N. Dinkins, Comptroller H. Carl McCall, Manhattan Borough President C. Virginia Fields and Senator Charles Schumer. The greetings were interspersed with musical performances by Opera Ebony, The Boys Choir of Harlem, Chuck Jackson and the Jazzmobile Summit, Opus 118 and the Harlem Sax Summit. Other dais guests included: Mayor Denis Archer (City of Detroit), Ms. Barbara Askins, Reverend John Carrington, Honorable Randy Daniels, Honorable Adam Clayton Powell IV, Reverend Dr. Wyatt T. Walker, State Senator David Patterson, Assemblyman, Keith Wright, Mr. Lloyd Williams, Honorable Stanley Gleaton, Assembly Denny Farrell, State Senator Olga Mendez, Councilman Stanley Michaels, Councilman William Perkins, Councilman Philip Reed, Reverend Adolph Roberts, Congressman Jose Serrano and Deborah Wright.

When former President Clinton got up to speak, the enthusiasm was overwhelming. Secretary of State Randy Daniels presented the former President with a Proclamation from Governor George Pataki, which proclaimed July 30th " Bill Clinton Day" in New York. Clinton began, "Thank you, now I feel like I'm home". He emotionally stated, "I'd like to personally thank one person who's not here", he pointed across the street at the Hotel Theresa, telling the crowd, "that's where (the late Commerce Secretary) Ron Brown grew up and I wish he was here today. President Clinton told the crowd that he was honored to be in Harlem, in New York City, in New York State. His new office was located at 55 West 125th Street on the 14th floor of the CAV Building, which has a panoramic city skyline view highlighted by the greenery of Central Park. He said that he wanted to be a good neighbor. He spoke of his commitment to help small businesses and how he would hate for us to be driven out of Harlem "on his account". He said, "What I'm gonna do here is promote economic equality, in the state and around the world. The great test of our future is whether we can take all of this division and turn it into something good. Harlem has always struck me as a place that was good and alive. Together we can be there for our neighbors and friends around the world".

President Clinton reminded the crowd about the initiation of the Empowerment Zone program, which was to contribute to the economic vitality of urban America, the decrease in the nation's welfare roll, and the employment boom, all of which occurred during his administration. President Clinton also talked about his ongoing AIDS initiative. He thanked Harlem for being with him "on the good days, as well as the dark days". "We live in a time when we need each other whether we know it or not".

President Clinton's remarks were brief, yet informative and he managed to add a touch of humor. As the program neared its end, he said that "while he had visited the Apollo, he had not yet played (saxophone) there. He shared (by this time, he was probably getting quite hungry) that one of his favorite restaurants is Sylvia's on 126th Street, where he had eaten several times, and he was glad it was right around the corner from his office.

President Clinton had preceded his arrival at the Harlem celebration with a letter addressed to "my fellow New Yorkers", which concluded with "I'm deeply grateful for the warm welcome I have received from my new neighbors, and I look forward to seeing all of you around town".

Well, I was very happy to hear that he wanted to be a good neighbor to us, he expressed concern and made a commitment to help small businesses and he said that he would hate for us to be driven out of Harlem on his account. "A test will be whether we can take all of this division and turn it into something good". Now I wonder, *had he possibly heard or sensed that we were going to be forced out?*

I was 1-1/2 blocks away. I tried to get his office to buy just paper from me, at the same or at a lower price than Staples, but some of his staff also were suffering from "Willie Lynch Syndrome". The young, African American woman in charge of his office might have felt it was important for the people at the large corporations to know that she was the President's choice. Like many others, President Clinton did not give his own staff the responsibility to find out who the African American business owners in Harlem were, what our businesses had been doing for years to create and maintain training and jobs for the people of Harlem, and to find out whether we were being included in getting support from the EZ.

I look at people today who seem honestly surprised that racial, sexual and class discrimination is happening daily, so it's possible President Clinton did not know what we were up against. We tried weekly to get his new office people in Harlem to buy something from Harlem Office Supply, Inc., less than two blocks away from them.

If that office had purchased from me, it would have forced decisions from City College on 138th Street in Harlem, Columbia University, the hospitals in Harlem and others to re-direct the flow of some of their dollars in support of the President's empowerment project. City College spends over a million dollars for paper per year. They were at that time spending that money and supporting upper class "white" neighborhoods in New Jersey. I was glad that former President Clinton was coming to Harlem and thought we would be helped, but staring me in the face was the same problem as always.

Several people have suggested that Clinton's presence in Harlem was the reason for the increase in rents for the African American business owners. I disagree with that. Sure, the fact that a former President taking an office in the neighborhood is worth something to the growth of the economy, but President Clinton came to Harlem after the Empowerment Zone's decisions were in place.

Mr. Clinton's office as a former president remains on the top floor of 55 West 125th Street. However, The William J. Clinton Foundation has moved most of its offices from Harlem to the Wall Street district. It is said that the move will give the foundation more space and will help cut costs as the rent will be cheaper than the $40 a square foot it pays in the Harlem building.

Chapter Eighteen

"New Harlem"

Established African American businesses could not get loans from the banks. If we had missed paying a Con-Edison light bill on time more than once, we were not considered a "real business". The existence of the Empowerment Zone came about because we were struggling. Now, the fact that we were struggling—and worse than before the EZ—was being used against us to deny us not only of any of the benefits of the EZ, but our homes, businesses, and community; and the cultural heritage that belonged to it.

A statement was made in the EZ's Introduction… "This mission is both one of rescue and development, salvaging and prevention".

Also in that statement is acknowledged the fact that Harlem people shouldered the burden of National neglect, yet had organized and worked to build economic empowerment. The funding of the EZ in Harlem acknowledged that we were in danger, and that we had the will, the vision and the capacity to reverse the trend if we were funded, and the systematic exclusion halted.

The EZ's Introduction also stated "the New York City EZ was chosen to target need and build capacity". It aimed at "targeting people in distress within an area that provided opportunities". The total number of people living in poverty in New York City exceeded the population of all but 7 US cities. There were several areas in New York City that met the criteria for EZ designation, but Harlem was considered to be strategically placed in the city and region. It mentioned the importance of the Harlem River, the Three Bridges, and the similarity of race and poverty in Harlem and the Bronx.

It further projected that the jobs that would be available to Harlem's many untrained residents would be service sector jobs, concentrated at the lower end of the labor market, paying minimum or near minimum wages. It was also noted that immigrants, who constitute a growing proportion of the population of New York and Harlem, were taking those jobs. And the published documents reflect also that the city leaders, and leaders in Harlem were well aware of this when they designed the strategic plan.

There were also statements made in the EZ materials, such as the Vision Statement it sent to the federal government, that suggested that Black and Hispanic families and children would need to have a program to teach them to have some "values and self respect". As if African Americans and Hispanics do not have values and self respect.

Wealth itself does not create values; but how the society deals with the wealth is an indicator of its values.

"Willie Lynch Syndrome" is a program for the "black slaves", the "servants and overseers" and the "wives and children" of the "gentlemen" it was presented to. It was to be applied as a total system.

Now, when I read the words in the EZ's Introduction, I see that they can be understood to mean a whole different thing than they would appear to. It seems that the "rescue", "salvage" and "development" of Harlem's human and economic resources have benefited the "gentry" of our city and nation. We were "targeted" as politically weak, and as an undesired ethnic group; and the program seems to have been implemented with the intention of preventing the economic, social and political empowerment of African Americans.

We are not unfamiliar with the line of thinking, whereby inhumane actions are justified by the idea that the opposed group are deficient in human "values" and are therefore not entitled to the resources that would fulfill their human need.

Harlem has institutions, churches, community organizations, hospitals, schools, entertainment centers, museums and cities, which mark and commemorate the lives and work of famous civil rights leaders, historians, scientists, innovators, teachers, musicians, artists and celebrities…all of which make Harlem more of a rich economic base for gentrification.

International tourists coming to New York must see Harlem. Keeping the African American cultural institutions grows the New York economy; but forcing the African American economic and cultural base out, and creating a permanent underclass of servants includes very few African Americans in that economic empowerment. The Harlem churches seem now to be entertainment centers for tourists. That's fine; but for the churches to take part in the process of the gentrification of the community is not fine.

Nor is it "fine" that gentrification has been the result of a program funded and mandated to enrich and empower a poor, *ethnic* community.

A number of organizations that worked on the plan that we understood would be sent to the government have reported that when they asked to see the final plan that was sent, they were denied. I never saw it either, and I wonder how we are supposed to feel assured that the plan that was mandated to be co-authored by us is actually the plan that was funded.

Relocation:

"Relocation", in a plan to economically empower the businesses and residents of a community, might have meant something like helping to relocate Copeland's restaurant when McDonald's Corp. decided to raise his rent after his $1.3 million improvement. Instead, there was a plan to relocate Harlem residents to upstate New York.

There was a model home on 125th Street between Madison and 1st Avenues. The EZ advertised w/ flyers, and in newspapers and radio for

Dorothy Hughes

people who would want to relocate out of Harlem. People could go into the model home, take a look and talk with an EZ representative about what kind of home the EZ would build for them. As part of the "empowerment of the community", a Harlem resident could apply and easily receive approval to be moved out of Harlem to upstate New York, which they claimed was just a few miles away.

In their introductory mission and responsibility it was stated that the EZ would change the economic, social, and physical conditions of persons, households, and neighborhoods in poverty and improve the overall quality of life for residents. At that time, low and middle-income families, seniors and young people could afford an apartment or home in Harlem; today it is nearly impossible.

For some time now, I've concentrated on the last of the African American business community in Harlem, but I'm interested in how many families of color have maintained residential ownership in Harlem and South Bronx in the areas identified as the zone.

For the purpose of the Empowerment Zone application, the zone area was grouped in sections: Central Harlem; East Harlem; West Harlem; Washington Heights/Inwood; Manhattanville; St. Nicholas Park; Hamilton Heights; Morningside; East Harlem Triangle; El Barrio; Central Barrio; Central Park North; 116th Street; Mt. Morris Park; and 125th Street.

The Empowerment Zone program priorities were stated to be:

1. "First source" hiring and procurement policy to build up EZ businesses and to put EZ residents to work.

2. To expand the range of economic opportunities available to EZ residents.

3. To prepare children and youth of the EZ for leadership work and for a productive future.

4. To ensure the availability and high quality of basic support services needed to help EZ residents realize their full productive potential.

5. To broaden the means by which residents are able to participate in decisions affecting the life of the community.

Which residents are enjoying these opportunities? When I lived in Harlem, my kids joked about the "exodus" of white people from the subway at the 96th Street stop, before it continued up to Harlem. If this was an Empowerment Zone for the people of Harlem, why do my children no longer live there, while their classmates from the private schools I worked to send them to, now own new Harlem brownstones and condos?

Chapter Nineteen

Wall Street

President Clinton moved his offices from Harlem to Wall Street in 2011 in search of cheaper rent. In 1997, as "New Harlem" began to take shape, I planned to "move" to Wall Street too; and to take as many African Americans and poor and disenfranchised people from Harlem with me, "From Sharecropping To Shareholding".

The whip on my back had torn the skin off my spirit, but I kept my head up. There were times that I would not sleep, I would spend all night listening to, or talking with Bob Law, one of the business voices of African Americans, on WWRL Radio. At that time we were working together with the "Buy Black" campaign that sought to curb the take-over of our community by educating the public that "where you spend your money is to whom you give your power". One Sunday, I was reading a copy of "The Black Chronicle", produced by Maloyd Ben Wilson, Jr. (owner & publisher, Wilson Group Network, Inc., Pennsylvania) and which I sold at my store. In it, was printed Marcus Garvey's speech, "Standing Up", and that day it became clear to me. Being an American with real hope for change, I wanted to spend time in Wall Street to see if I could see what others felt. Harlem is only ten miles from Wall Street. Why were we not participating in the process of generating and enjoying wealth?

I had to find a way that I could direct Harlem's African American families to economic empowerment daily. I knew that we were being used to pass money, though making it seem as if we were reaping the benefits.

The EZ had been funded and we were still suffering with poverty, illness, homelessness, bad schools, police brutality, no health care, racism, sexism and classism.

I decided that Sunday evening that I would go to Wall Street the next day, choose a starting point and become educated about stocks. I was raging inside from having read that Wall Street was named after the city council had instructed a team of slaves to build a wall to separate the area for trading slaves from the scene of the removal of the bodies of those who had died on board the ships on the way from Africa to America.

I took a walk down Maiden Lane. I had read that this street was named "Maiden Lane" because it was where the enslaved black women could be sexually used and had been paraded down the street to be chosen by the white men in waiting. I wanted to change that image in my own mind and in the minds of any others who might have read this—and going forward; the students of Harlem should not have that image blocking their thoughts on what Wall Street could represent for them.

The amount of capital African Americans spend goes from Wall Street to take care of every one except us, so I wanted to know how we could become involved. It seemed the right time. I knew that I wanted to learn and teach "Economic Empowerment 101". I wanted to use the opportunity that I had had for a few years now to work with children and their parents on economic empowerment. If I could understand the stock system myself, I would take thousands of African Americans to Wall Street as shareholders, standing up! Alive. And so I began.

That Monday, in February 1996, after perusing the area for a couple of hours, I walked into an office building that looked interesting. As fate had it, I decided to start in the middle of the building, so I went to the third floor. I didn't know what I wanted, but when the receptionist asked that question, I answered, "Could I use your ladies' room?" She said, "Sure, it's locked, but someone will open it for you". To my surprise, the woman she called to my aid was someone I had spent quite a bit of time with a few months earlier.

Doris had been unjustly fired from Harlem Hospital because she would not mistreat a person that her supervisors didn't like. When she came to me at the Harlem Office Supply, we did not just make her copies and do her typing. I saw that she needed to talk and remove the anger and pain. So we had gone for coffee while her work was being done. And now, here she was in an office on Wall Street…this was a great sign. I thanked God, and told her that I needed someone to tell me about Wall Street, and how I could get Harlem families involved. I told her some of my plans and she invited me into their conference room.

About 10 minutes later she came in with a young man, whom she introduced to me as her son, Vernon Gibson, a Wall Street Financial Consultant and CEO with 21st Century Finance Co. He thanked me for helping his mom when she needed help. I discussed with him my views on how to create wealth among people left out of the economic mainstream and that day I learned more from Vernon than I had any of the economics and business courses in which I had enrolled in previous years at The College of New Rochelle and Fordham University. He invited me back to learn more as I worked the idea of Economic Empowerment in Harlem. A few days later, I began training with his firm on Wall Street.

Wall Street Financial Consultant Vernon Gibson with Dorothy Hughes at a conference where they participated in discussions on "how to create wealth among African Americans."

After many years of struggling, as a visionary/entrepreneur, I was ready to enter the study of the economic mainstream in Wall Street. I see Wall Street as one of the vehicles through which people can achieve self economic empowerment. The purpose for my training was to learn first-hand how Wall Street operated and how I could assist others by introducing them to the world of stocks, and how to economically empower them. Once learned, I took the information I had, and made it available to adults and children in Harlem, affording them the opportunity to become economically empowered.

I learned that many families and their friends celebrated the births of children by buying or switching stock into their names to gain a position of paying no taxes on those assets for eighteen years. This practice has helped many families with children and ensured the children will be financially set to attend college and buy their first homes—giving them a tax free "head start" that reaches all the way into adulthood. It became very important to me to organize stock clubs and family groups to learn about the process and "put stock" in their futures.

The first group of children who became HOS shareholders .

Dorothy speaking at a 1998 shareholders meeting

Harlem Office Supply, Inc. (HOS) was opened and based in Harlem, in 1985. I began it with a vision and mission to involve inner-city people in the economic mainstream, where they had been left out. The process included teaching and practicing consumer ownership of my company, HOS, Inc. through a stock offering, by selling shares in my business to people in communities throughout New York.

Harlem Office Supply, Inc.

STOCK OFFERING

"From Sharecropping to Shareholding - Bridging the Gap"

6. East 125th Street
New York, NY. 10035
(212) 427-3540 Tel.
(212) 427-3816 Fax

---

100 SHARE MINIMUM FOR ADULTS
50 SHARE MINIMUM
FOR CHILDREN UNDER 18
(Cash, Check, Money Order, Visa, MasterCard)

Buy H.O.S. Inc. Stock now and celebrate the year 2000 as the year we close the economic gap in America and put our children in charge of their economic future!

Name: _____
Address: _____
City: _____
State: _____ Zip: _____
Phone: ( ) _____
# of Shares _____ $ Enclosed: _____
Include **$5.00** for mailing of certificate
SS# _____
Ck/M.O. _____ Or please bill my MasterCard or Visa
CC# _____ Exp. Date: _____
Signature _____

Please make checks payable to:
Harlem Office Supply, Inc.
Stock Offering

HARLEM OFFICE SUPPLY, INC. (212) 427-3540
6 EAST 125th STREET (212) 427-3615
NEW YORK, NY. 10035 Fax (212) 427-3816

FROM SHARECROPPING TO SHAREHOLDING...

Historically, black people have been invited to participate in the economic life of America, but not necessarily to benefit from that participation.

Today, African-American and Hispanic consumers spend over 500 billion dollars annually, but this major participation in the American economy benefits us and our children shamefully little, as "sharecropper" economics continues to plague our communities.

WHERE YOU PUT YOUR MONEY IS WHERE YOU GIVE YOUR POWER

It is not that we have the power, it is that we as a community are not empowered. We do not hold the power — it slips through our fingers at a rate of $500 Billion a year.

OWNERSHIP:
BRIDGING THE GAP

Ownership creates better lifestyles and a sound community infrastructure. Black business represents actual black economic and social power, and the ability to sustain healthy,thriving Black communities.

H.o.s, Inc. and its over 7000 shareholders invite you to join us in bridging the gap between power and empowerment; between mere participation and real emancipation...

73

Dorothy P. Hughes
PRESIDENT AND C.E.O.

Harlem Office Supply, Inc.'s management team is headed by the Company's President and C.E.O. Dorothy Pitman Hughes. The Founder of the Company, she has long been dedicated to creating better economic opportunities for her community, and has a long and varied history as a developer, organizer and director of successful enterprises. Ms. Hughes has devoted the past 10 years, and a major financial commitment to the planning, development and expansion of H.O.S., Inc.

Ms. Hughes founded and organized NYC's Agency for Child Development, has owned and operated three day care centers , sponsored a successful youth entrepreneur apprentice project and spent three years as a public speaker on the university circuit.

Ms. Hughes is the first African-American woman to become a member of the Stationers' Association of New York. She is also a member of the Harlem Business Alliance, Black Women Enterprises, The National Black Women's Political Congress, The National Council of Negro Women, The National Organization for Women and Women Initiating Self Empowerment.

PRIVATE STOCK OFFERING

Harlem Office Supply, Inc. is offering shares in the Company to the members of our inner city and rural communities under the Securities Exchange Commission's (SEC) 504 Regulation D plan.

This is a Private Stock Offering with which the Company and its shareholders can expand the business and raise the value of its stock in order to take the business to the Stock Market, or "go public".

It is a process by which shareholders invest in the success of the business while at the same time insuring its success, and ultimately, the success of their communities, their families and themselves.

H.o.s. Inc.'s expansion plan to open Campus Business Centers on 106 Black College campuses will culminate in taking the company to Wall Street with at least 51% Black ownership.

H.O.S. Inc.'s shareholders will themselves be the major underwriters of the stock and will therefore be the main benefactors, insuring that more of the money we spend in our communities will stay in our communities.

The average Black College campus spends $4 million per year on office supplies, printing and copying services. As each of these new Campus Business Centers are erected, the students faculty, parents and residents of the surrounding communities as well as all H.O.S. Inc. shareholders will reap the benefits of that annual expenditure ending the cycle of Black dollars being funneled out of our communities to feed the families, and support the communities and social agendas of large, white owned corporations and their shareholders.

IT'S TIME TO EMPOWER OURSELVES! BUY STOCK AND INVEST IN YOUR FUTURE

- *Harlem office supply, Inc. will furnish its shareholders with annual financial statements prepared by independent certified public accountants as well as unaudited quarterly financial reports.*

- *Prior to this offering there has been no public market for any securities of the Company.*

Chapter Twenty

Ownership and Power

On May 15, 1997 the Offering Memorandum was completed for Harlem Office Supply, Inc., and the filing process began. (See Appendix A)

In July, 1997 we completed the process of registering and filing the Offering Memorandum with the State of New York Department of Law. Issuer Statement, (Section 359-CBus.Law), New York form M-11, (Rev.5/90), file number 5279392 was filed on July 8, 1997. Registered through the N.Y. State Attorney General Office. All documents were reviewed and filed by Ms. Joan Greg and Mr. Gary O'Connor of the Attorney General's Office.

Filing was complete with Offering Literature. The Filing Fee ($800) was paid at the Bureau of Investor Protection and Securities New York, Department of Law, located at 120 Broadway, New York, New York 10271.

(Offering Memorandum: Files May 15, 1997—Harlem Office Supply, Inc., offering shares at a price of $1.00 per share. Filed N.Y. form M-11, Rev.5/90. July 8, 1997—Approved by the state of New York, Department of Law, Section 3.59-C, General Business Law for the purpose of Issuer offering stock. Total amount of offering, $500,000. Filing fee remitted to Bureau of Investor Protection and Securities, New York Department of Law, 120 Broadway, New York, 10271, both departments falling under the office of the State Attorney General, Eliot Spitzer.)

The offering was approved by the State of New York Attorney General's Office and according to the Securities Act of 1933, everything was in place for Harlem Office Supply, Inc., to qualify for Wall Street. The State of New York provided Harlem Office Supply, Inc., with its first 500 Stock Certificates and HOS was now in place to sell 500 shares.

With the assistance of Amy Culver, Franchise Tax Specialist, Harlem Office Supply, Inc. completed all of the filing requirements, appointed a Board of Directors, hired Attorneys with experience in working with Stocks and began selling shares of stocks to my company.

The Board of Directors was made up of the following persons:
Dorothy Hughes / Chairman
Tony Jenkins / Vice President
Lee Lancaster / Treasurer
Joseph Palmer / Director
Delethia Marvin / Director
Samuel Peabody / Director

Our Legal Team:
Corey M. Turner, Esq., Brooklyn, NY
Anthony Richards, Esq., Nyack, NY
Marilyn Ward Ford, Esq., Quinnipiac College School of Law
Peter G. Eikenberry, Esq. New York City, Wall Street
Edward Fordham, Esq., Harlem, NY

With our company mission in place, we made the community aware of the offer by advertisement, had meetings in schools, spoke at churches, and rented a theater on 125th Street. At a Harlem theater, in one evening we sold $85,000 worth of shares. At this time 2,300 children became shareholders and we eventually sold shares to over 7,000 people at $1.00 per share.

Now a database listing of 7,063 people were poised to become shareholders in the first Harlem-based business to go public. The decision was made to merge with Hand Brand Distribution Inc., a firm that was currently being traded over the counter.

Prior to the merger announcement, we made sure everything was in order and being handled according to the rules and regulations of the U.S Securities and Exchange Commission, (SEC), 504 Reg-D. This is the regulation of the SEC, which allows small businesses to raise capital by offering stock shares. By following these guidelines, the organization was formed and the plans for the merger were put in place. The plan was to ultimately raise $2,000,000 by offering stock for $1.00 per share.

We held a press conference and luncheon in a Wall Street historical restaurant, where we announced the merger of Harlem Office Supply, Inc., and Hand Brand Distribution, Inc., a firm already traded publicly on Wall Street. With this transaction, I was about to become the first African-American female from Harlem to be President of a publicly traded business operation.

Hand Brand Distribution Inc. is a publisher of family-oriented, health-related periodicals and distributes nutritional supplements. The two companies exchanged 500,000 shares of common stock to complete the merger of the two companies.

By joining forces together, the two companies wished to reach a common goal. In an article in the Amsterdam News, (vol.92 No.23 June 7-13, 2001), John M. Taggart, president of Hand Brand Distributions, said he was excited about the merger because his firm had "similar visions to economically empower people who have been left out of the economic mainstream." To this statement, I added, "And I think we should do it within this century".

With the announcement made and the Letter of Intent signed, the merger of the two companies was becoming a reality and the people of the community were going to know the true meaning of financial freedom. But we were stopped by Eliot Spitzer, the State Attorney General.

July 18, 2001 I received an order to "Cease and Desist" with the merger while the State Attorney's office conducted an inquiry into the legality of the merger. Due to this public inquiry and alleged wrongdoings on my part and on the part of Harlem Office Supplies, Inc., my integrity and that of the organization were put into question. Caught in the middle were the seven thousand shareholders, wondering what was going to happen to them and their dreams.

Then State Attorney General, and later Governor of the State of New York, Eliot Spitzer, who became famous because of his recent exposure as a participant in a prostitution ring, with the stroke of a pen, destroyed what I had worked 30 years to build.

In 2001 after the inquiry was complete, I received notification that the State Attorney's office could find no wrongdoing on my part or by the organization. However, by the time the witch-hunt was over, the reputation of the integrity of both the organization and myself had been effectively destroyed, along with the dreams of the men, women and children invested in the company.

The rent for the space on 125th Street, where Harlem Office Supply was located, had been increased from $4000 to $21,000 per month in 2000; and neither the business nor the organization could survive. With the cost of the legal fees and the increased cost to operate the business, I was forced to sell both my homes in an attempt to pay legal fees to keep my integrity and the hopes of the people intact.

Even though Harlem Office Supply, Inc. dissolved, we have kept the stock registered under Harlem Business Development Corp., in the hope that one day we will be able to continue with our mission to bring economic empowerment to the shareholders.

The action of one man has negatively affected the lives of thousands of people. The loss of the merger not only affected my shareholders and me and my children, both personally and financially, but an entire community. With the stroke of a pen, this one man was able to end the upward movement of a community that could have enabled and empowered not only this generation, but also many generations to come.

The sale of shares between 1997 and 2000 was done based on the Securities Act of 1933, afforded by Rule 504 Regulation D. Several successful companies have grown their business through Rule 504 Reg. D, which, I have been told, was changed after I used it, so that no one could use it in the way I did. I'm just saying… ***It looks like ethnic cleansing.***

Chapter Twenty-one

A New Act

Twelve years after I received the letter from Eliot Spitzer to cease and desist the sale of stock, something familiar and very interesting has occurred. President Obama's recent JOBS Act is an amendment to the 1933 Act, which will allow for "re-opening American capital markets to emerging growth companies". The new JOBS Act, supported by both Democrats and Republicans, is now a law of the land. It will do what we were trying to do—bring people into economic empowerment.

Here is a summary of how the bill works, taken from an article in the *New York Times*:

> *The JOBS Act would designate a new category of "emerging growth" companies that could conduct initial public offerings of stock while being exempt from certain financial disclosure and governance requirements for up to five years. It would also provide a new form of financing to small companies. Through crowd-funding, or the sale of small amounts of stock to many individuals, companies could solicit equity investments through the Internet or elsewhere, raising up to $1 million annually without being required to register the shares for public trading with the Securities and Exchange Commission.*
>
> *Supporters see it as a breakthrough for entrepreneurs who hope to build an enterprise around sometimes offbeat ideas without having to sell them to larger companies.*

Under the JOBS bill, companies with up to $1 billion in annual revenue would be free to ignore—for their first five years as a public company—regulations that were put in place after the end of the dot-com bubble and the collapse of Enron.

Among them are requirements to hire an independent outside auditor to attest to a company's internal financial controls and restrictions on how financial analysts interact with investment bankers in promoting a company's stock.

The bill also allows some companies to advertise for investors in almost any medium, a provision that skeptical regulators contend will mainly benefit the sale of worthless securities by brokerage firms.

Senate Democrats did add some investor protections that were ratified by the House. Senators added a provision to ensure that any company using crowd-funding methods must still file some basic information with the securities commission, including the names of directors, officers and holders of more than 20 percent of the company's shares, plus a description of the business and its financial condition.

Companies seeking to raise $100,000 or less must also provide tax returns and a financial statement certified by a company principal; those raising up to $500,000 must provide financial statements that are reviewed by an independent public accountant.

The Senate also inserted requirements that intermediaries seeking to help companies raise money through crowd-funding must register with the commission, make sure investors are advised of the risks they are taking, and take measures to prevent fraud.

Remarks by President Obama at JOBS Act Bill Signing (April 5, 2012)

One of the great things about America is that we are a nation of doers—not just talkers, but doers. We think big. We take risks. And we believe that anyone with a solid plan and a willingness to work hard can turn even the most improbable idea into a successful business. So ours is a legacy of Edisons and Graham Bells, Fords and Boeings, of Googles and of Twitters. This is a country that's always been on the cutting edge. And the reason is that America has always had the most daring entrepreneurs in the world.

Some of them are standing with me today. When their ideas take root, we get inventions that can change the way we live. And when their businesses take off, more people become employed because, overall, new businesses account for almost every new job that's created in America.

Now, because we're still recovering from one of the worst recessions in our history, the last few years have been pretty tough on entrepreneurs. Credit has been tight. And no matter how good their ideas are, if an entrepreneur can't get a loan from a bank or backing from investors, it's almost impossible to get their businesses off the ground. And that's why back in September (2011), and again in my State of the Union, I called on Congress to remove a number of barriers that were preventing aspiring entrepreneurs from getting funding. And this is one useful and important step along that journey.

Here's what's going to happen because of this bill. For business owners who want to take their companies to the next level, this bill will make it easier for you to go public. And that's a big deal because going public is a major step towards expanding and hiring more workers. It's a big deal for investors as well, because public companies operate with greater oversight and greater transparency.

And for start-ups and small businesses, this bill is a potential game changer. Right now, you can only turn to a limited group of investors—including banks and wealthy individuals—to get funding. Laws that are nearly eight decades old make it impossible for others to invest. But a lot has changed in 80 years, and it's time our laws did as well. Because of this bill, start-ups and small business will now have access to a big, new pool of potential investors—namely, the American people. For the first time, ordinary Americans will be able to go online and invest in entrepreneurs that they believe in.

Of course, to make sure Americans don't get taken advantage of, the websites where folks will go to fund all these start-ups and small businesses will be subject to rigorous oversight. The SEC is going to play an important role in implementing this bill. And I've directed my administration to keep a close eye as this law goes into effect and to provide me with regular updates.

It also means that, to all the members of Congress who are here today, I want to say publicly before I sign this bill, it's going to be important that we continue to make sure that the SEC is properly funded, just like all our other regulatory agencies, so that they can do the job and make sure that our investors get adequate protections.

This bill represents exactly the kind of bipartisan action we should be taking in Washington to help our economy. I've always said that the true engine of job creation in this country is the private sector, not the government. Our job is to help our companies grow and hire. That's why I pushed for this bill. That's why I know that the bipartisan group of legislators here pushed for this bill. That's why I've cut taxes for small businesses over 17 times. That's why every day I'm fighting to make sure America is the best place on Earth to do business.

Our economy has begun to turn a corner, but we've still got a long way to go. We've still got a lot of Americans out there who are looking for a job or looking for a job that pays better than the one that they've got. And we're going to have to keep working together so that we can keep moving the economy forward.

But I've never been more confident about our future. And the reason is because of the American people. Some of the folks beside me here today are a testimony to that. Day after day, they're out there pitching investors. Some meetings go well; some meetings don't go so well. That's true for me, too. But no matter what, they keep at it. And who knows, maybe one of them will be the next Bill Gates or Steve Jobs or Mark Zuckerberg. And one of them may be the next entrepreneur to turn a big idea into an entire new industry. That's the promise of America. That's what this country is all about.

So if these entrepreneurs are willing to keep giving their all, the least Washington can do is to help them succeed. I plan to do that now by proudly signing this bill.

Thank you very much, everybody.

President Obama has given us something to work with. But how we work with it will make the difference. What we have to watch out for is that we don't separate people out again.

During the earlier working stages of the gentrification process in Harlem, those of us who were protesting, and working to keep our businesses and our homes in Harlem, should have been joined by our African American leaders. They did not join us. Instead they became the instruments for gentrifying Harlem. Those of us who were working, and would have continued to work for the actual economic empowerment of Harlem were targeted for removal—making Harlem so weak that the economic empowerment of Harlem's people may no longer be possible without a movement to "Occupy Harlem".

Chapter Twenty-two

How Gentrification Feels

My two businesses (Harlem Office Supply, Inc. and the Sojourner Truth Bed & Breakfast) were unique for Harlem; they were both service-oriented and had the potential of creating a model for economic empowerment. I also made it clear to everyone that it was our intention to do just that.

People could participate in weekly or monthly events relating to economic empowerment by contacting us at Harlem Office Supply, Inc. All of this work toward empowerment was going on at the same time. I have always seen the connection that helping others helps me. People are now calling this "paying it forward".

I realized that to help build my business, I would need to communicate with as many people as possible. Other people had shown me the need to get together to network. Bob Law, the radio announcer and businessman, had introduced me to a process of visiting the local businesses to help insure their ability to pay rent and/or Con Edison (electric). At the network gatherings I hosted on the first Thursday in each month at the Cotton Club in Harlem, each business owner was asked to take the stage and speak for five minutes about their business, announce the number of the table they would be sitting at and invite the room to do business with them. We always had a guest speaker who would give a lecture on self economic empowerment; and often, even when they were not scheduled as the keynote speakers, they came and spoke. During one of the most successful Thursday meetings we had, we traded about two hundred thousand dollars in business.

Our monthly attendees and speakers included: Rev. Al Sharpton, Bob Law, John Beatty, writer, Gloria Dulan Wilson; Mr. Copeland, Florence Rice, Dee Dee's Card Shop and many others. We were getting to know each other well and supporting each other's businesses.

As far as I know, I was the first African American female to own an office supply store in Harlem. Harlem Office Supply had been in existence since 1985 and was incorporated in 1992 in New York State. It was registered as a minority business and was eligible for several federal, State and city legislated financial programs aimed at economic empowerment. But we were faced with racism, sexism and classism.

I had to fight with the industry in order to buy products to sell. The large corporations would not sell to me. I knew it was racism that was blocking me, so I hired an 18-year-old white male to go with me to the wholesale suppliers and buy for me.

I had gone to one company with a list of supplies I wanted to order. They quoted me an order estimate of $10,300 and said they would only take a cashier's check from me. I went back with Keith (making sure they weren't aware we were together) and he was able to get a quote on the exact same list for less than $7,000. Not only did he get a lower quote, but he paid with a personal check! Of course we had to go directly to his bank to cover it. His check was not even questioned.

I accepted that insult, and all the others in order to help the community to bring in the Empowerment Zone, which promised capitalization of our small businesses as well as bringing in large corporations to help with sustainability. I believed that we would grow the economy; instead my rent was raised. I was forced to leave that store, but I immediately opened another store two blocks east. Then choices had to be made: do I pay the taxes? (which I now call "taxes to be poor") or do I take a chance on staying in business and pay the taxes later?

The people in power decided to use the tax issue to close my business down; the door was locked. I called the Honorable Percy Sutton, attorney and former co-owner of Inner City Broadcasting, and Susan Taylor, former Editor-in-Chief of Essence Magazine. The locks were removed in 24 hours. I diversified my business plan to include copy services, books, art, economic workshops, stock market information for adults and children and general information on the people who were selling out Harlem.

As I concentrated on what was not being brought out about the EZ, and who was doing what, I learned that there was more to what was going on in Harlem than I thought. So I started a local project to economically educate parents and their children that "where you spend your money is to whom you give your power" through a stock program. One of my daughters wrote to Oprah Winfrey to say I was helping parents to start stock clubs, buying stock at $1.00 per share. And I appeared on her show.

The "Cease and Desist" letter did not come without Spitzer hearing from people who knew me contacting him. A few years ago, Gloria Steinem spoke with him and I know that Samuel Peabody spoke with him. Sam also wrote a letter to Spitzer about what I was experiencing in Harlem; but I now believe that Spitzer and people who worked for him had an interest in moving me out of Harlem.

SAMUEL P. PEABODY
990 FIFTH AVENUE
NEW YORK, NEW YORK 10021-0141

1/10/09

Dear Governor Spitzer,

Dorothy Pitman Hughes is a remarkable lady whom I've known and supported since the early 60's. She has spent all those years and more as a community organizer in Harlem, mostly on her own. Her mission has been to educate her neighbors to show they are capable of doing much more for themselves in raising their quality of life. She has been doing this even while working to run Harlem Office Supply and in spite of her ongoing financial problems.

Even today, where she now lives in Florida, Dorothy is continuing to teach her neighbors that they are able to do much more to improve their lives.

As an educator, I've been involved with several non-profit education programs and have the very highest regard for this lady.

I am not sure what you are able to do for her at this time other than plead her case to someone who is able to help her. Should you have any questions, please feel free to call me. I can best be reached during the morning. Not that you should remember, but we met briefly a couple of years ago through Barbara Lee Jiamordstein.

Sincerely,

Sam Peabody

One day, I got a telephone call from a woman who worked in the Harlem Office of the New York Attorney General, she asked me for the list of people who had bought shares. I asked why she needed the list, and explained to her that I could not disclose it. She then demanded the list, reminding me that she was in the Attorney General's Office.

I requested that she put her request in writing and told her that my lawyers would get back to her. That same day, I got a call from Claude D. Tims, of that same office, telling me that I had to come to their 125th Street office that afternoon or they would come and close us down. I called Attorney Marilyn W. Ford who advised me to go.

After waiting thirty minutes, a person introducing herself as Ms. Raysor asked me to come into her office. Claude was seated there and I was asked how many investors I had. I was also asked how much money I had in the bank. When I told Ms. Raysor, she said "I know you are just joking". I told her I wasn't, and she then said one more thing, "How did you get all up in Oprah's Show? I'm from Chicago and I couldn't get on her show." "I don't know how I got there", I answered. She then told me she wanted that list by 3:00 P.M. the next day and a copy of my last bank statement "or else."

I asked her why she wanted the list. She explained that it was not any of my business. I called Attorney Ford, and she called Ms. Raysor and arranged a meeting for the next week. When we met the next week, my attorney explained that the list would not be available unless by some legal means. Ms. Raysor questioned me: "How can you do all of this? You are not a lawyer." My lawyer answered, "She doesn't need to be lawyer, I'm her lawyer". Ms Ford then proceeded to turn the pages in a very large law book and read something to Ms. Raysor that I did not understand. Apparently, Ms. Raysor had not realized that if it was possible for her to become a lawyer, it was also possible for Ms. Ford.

Ms. Raysor's power as a person hired to carry out the policies of the Attorney General's Office may have given her some sense of control as she was getting paid to exploit my company. She may have rejoiced in that. I was the black woman with no college degree. But I was unwilling to follow the program of allowing her to "whip" me for her master. You will note the political shift that has taken place in Harlem since African American business was forced out. Ms. Raysor was able to be the kind of "boss" that people would have to do what she said or they might get punched.

Soon after, I was shocked to receive a letter from Claude D. Tims at the Harlem Office of the Attorney General stating that there was a complaint from Herbert Jenkins and Ramon Bellido, claiming that Harlem Office Supply, Inc., had failed to declare dividends or issue a financial report. There was no notice of when the report was supposed to be filed for dividends, and there was nothing stated about when I was supposed to report to Jenkins and Bellido—the stock law did not require me to report to shareholders except when there was a full meeting called.

I learned that Mr. Jenkins worked as a cleaner for the Harlem State Office Building. It was my understanding that he was told that he would no longer be qualified to keep his job with them if he owned stock with us. He was advised to request his money back ($10.00). He was also told that the Attorney General's Office would make the request. I did not know him before that request.

With Ramon, I did know his situation because I knew his mom. Ramon has a workable mental problem; he had been one of the persons that I worked with for as many as 7 years, and he was a classmate of one of my daughters. He had been cared for at my daycare center on 80th Street, and then at the Westside Community Alliance Youth program when he was a child.

I let Ramon come to these programs as a way of helping him and his mom. One day he was giving out flyers for me when he said, "I want stock too". I had given him a job for a couple of hours to pass out the flyers and I paid him, in part, by buying $10.00 in stock for him. I filled out the paperwork and gave him his certificate. He was very, very happy to be treated as other stockholders were. So, it surprised me when I learned that he was the person who filed a complaint against me and the company. I requested a copy of the complaint files but have never received it.

One day, after these incidents, I tried to reach Claude D. Tims and found that he had been fired from the Harlem State Office. *I wondered if he thought this might be "Ethnic Cleansing".* I continued with the request that the "complaining" stockholders should both be refunded their $10.00 and as this was done, Ramon cried. I told him that if the State would approve of it we would put stock in his mom's name for him.

At that time, with this kind of nonsense, I could not believe that this would be serious, but it was.

We had an election coming up, Eliot Spitzer was running for Governor, and it was mentioned that Senator Patterson could be Lieutenant Governor, if Spitzer could win. Congressman Charles Rangel was running for Congress again and for the Chair of the Ways and Means Committee, a big congressional office; and Adam Clayton Powell IV was running against him.

The rights to control Harlem were at the forefront of Harlem Politics, and Charlie felt that I might work to support Adam. I have continued over the years to respect what the Powell family has done for Harlem so far. Not being such a quiet person, I probably come across as one who could be of real help to the person that I felt was really for the people of Harlem.

The possibility of economically empowering African Americans and other people of color in Harlem would have also socially and politically empowered them, thus the move was made to stop those of us who had real economic empowerment in mind.

African American business owners had had to fight to get into the EZ meetings, or to get a meeting with our political representatives. We wanted help so that we could create real economic empowerment in our community. The leadership told us that they were trying to find ways to insure more participation of the "larger community", and that they were focusing on "training" and "jobs". We were aware of how things operate in a racist, classist society. It changes nothing if you have skills but are not hired because you're a person of color, or not in the "social class" to be hired. Beside that, we were not just talking about "jobs"; we were talking about ownership. The jobs-focused model has nothing to do with economic empowerment, but everything to do with creating a permanent underclass of servants.

When W.I.S.E. was formed we requested a meeting with Congressman Rangel. After weeks of requests for a meeting, his secretary asked for a written request and explanation of what we would discuss. We had a couple of days to get it to his office. An appointment was given, and two days later we were told he could not meet with us then and, when possible, they would call us with another date. For three weeks we waited for a phone call; then I visited the congressman in his office and organized my own meeting with him. I called all of the women of W.I.S.E., gave them the time and date, and they met me there.

When we arrived, we were asked to wait outside in the lobby. One of the businesswomen was also a Minister. After waiting twenty minutes, I asked her to pray with us, and she did. There were people coming out of their offices, coming up on the elevators, coming to see what was going on; she was good and loud, and we "witnessed" just as we would have in church. Congressman Rangel soon sent for us. It was after this that the Congressman finally agreed to let us be represented on the EZ committee.

In Conclusion

Ethnic Cleansing

Tactics of "ethnic cleansing" include "intimidation, forced expulsion, and destruction or removal of physical vestiges of the ethnic group". Also, it is customary to under-capitalize the ethnic group so that physical vestiges cannot be built in the territory in places of worship, cultural institution buildings, or historic sites. In the case of Harlem there had been, for years before the emergence of the EZ, a Small Business Administration. But if you were African American, you got no help from them.

Another tactic of "ethnic cleansing" is that the "desired" community is made to believe that the "undesired" ethnic group is a hostile community. They are also "motivated to believe a doctrine that claims that the ethnic group is literally unclean, as in the case of the Jews of medieval Europe".

When gentrification was mentioned in an EZ committee meeting, the leaders would tell us that it was not a replacement, it was diversity-integration. I remember how it was when we lived under "Jim Crow" in Georgia. Before integration, we African Americans owned our own businesses. We ran "total" communities. We bought from each other and we served each other well. We did not cheat each other; rather, we gave more to each other, making sure that every family in our community was taken care of. As "white" business began to see the benefits of "integration", we allowed what they were *selling*—the idea that they were better equipped to serve us than we—to become part of our mindset.

We witnessed the almost complete closing down of our own businesses in all of the states where we had integration.

According to numerous verdicts, forced performed ethnic cleansing of territories is planned by the political leadership in order to bring ethnically "racial" classes and economically desired groups to a particular territory. The local leaders become the planners and at the same time, it is necessary, they became "the investigators" of the Ethnic Cleansing.

The plan in Harlem has been successful in eliminating citizens' support for resistance by the removal of African American business owners. Class, sex and skin color were used to contribute to a long-term fear of protest. Could this be treated as a war crime?

Where could we take the Harlem case to find out if the plan for the empowerment of Harlem was really a plan for the ethnic cleansing of Harlem? If we had been aware of what was really happening to us we might have taken our problem to the OSCE or to the UN general assembly for a resolution.

In the years that I have been actively involved in the struggle for African Americans to have equality in economic opportunity and our rights to social and political power, it has not happened. I want to live, not just exist in the country I was born in.

Economic, social and political disparity is an ill. It is proven that regardless of how rich or poor any nation is, the health and happiness of *all* of its citizens depends on whether or not there is economic parity. The disparity itself is "self-fueling", as Willie Lynch put it, and causes confusion because it is so un-natural.

It is telling that a society that holds itself as being a post-racist society also holds the belief that there are certain ethnic groups within it who have less of the "values" and "self respect" required to live at what the society itself would designate as "human standards".

It seems to me that because—by our existence, our goals, and our long-standing focus on training our youth—the existing Harlem businesses were operating in opposition to the Harlem "take-over", and it was viewed that we therefore had to be eliminated. We did not go quietly. We fought; we struggled, we held on as long as we could. We were defeated.

Here in America, where inequality has been the name of the game for a long time, people have ingested the concept that the winner of a fight is righteous by virtue of his victory. But if the fight is one-sided, and the gains made by cheating, theft and brutality—where is there any real justification for his reaping all the rewards? Those who benefit, and even some who don't, will look for justification because everyone wants to feel they are correct in their thoughts and actions.

Those people who decide to take responsibility now, to make change happen, must understand that their past responsibilities might have been to continue racism, sexism, classism, and exploitation. I encourage you to look deeply. I have, and...*I'm just saying, it looks like Ethnic Cleansing.*

Appendix A

Harlem Office Supply, Inc. Offering Memorandum and Subscription Agreement

HARLEM OFFICE SUPPLY, INC.
A maximum of 500,000 Shares
Offering Price - $1.00 per Share

Harlem Office Supply, Inc. (the "Company") hereby offers (the "Offering") a maximum of 500,000 Shares (each a "Share and collectively the Shares") of the Company's common stock, par value $0.001 per share ("Common Stock") at an offering price of $1.00 per Share has been arbitrarily determine by the Company and bears no relationship to the assets or book value of the Company or any other recognized criteria of value.

Prior to this Offering there has been no public market for any securities of the Company and no assurances can be given that a market will develop for the Shares or, if developed, that it will be maintained after the Offering.

This Offering is being made pursuant to the exemption from the registration provisions of the Securities Act of 1933, as amended, afforded by Rule 504 of Regulation D promulgated thereunder and state small corporate offering registration provisions. Pursuant to said Rule 504, said Rule 504, the securities sold hereby will not be subject to any limitations on the resale thereof under Federal law. Such securities will, however, be subject to limitations on the offer and sale and the resale of the Shares imposed by the blue sky laws of individual states.

THESE SECURITIES HAVE NOT BEEN APPROVED OR DISAPPROVED BY ANY FEDERAL OR STATE SECURITIES AGENCY NOR HAS ANY AGENCY REVIEWS OR PASSED UPON THE ACCURACY OR ADEQUACY OF THIS DISCLUSRE STATEMENT. ANY REPRESENTATION TO THE CONTRARY IS A CRIMINAL OFFENSE.

THE SECURITIES OFFERED HEREBY ARE HIGHLY SPECULATIVE, INVOLVE A HIGH DEGREE OF RISK AND SHOULD BE PURCHASED ONLY BY PERSONS WHO CAN AFFORD TO LOSE THEIR ENTIRE INVESTMENT. ACCORDINGLY, INVESTORS MUST RELY UPON THEIR OWN EXAMINATION OF THIS OFFERING AND THE COMPANY IN MAKING AN INVESTMENT DECISION. SEE "RISK FACTORS"

	Price to Public	Underwriting Discounts (1)	Proceeds to Company (2)
Per Share............ $1.00		$0.10	$0.90
Total Maximum 500,000Share............ $500,000		$50,000	$450,000

(see footnotes on following page)

The date of this Offering Memorandum is May 15, 1997

96

FOOTNOTES:

(1)   The Shares are being offered directly by the Company on a "best efforts" basis. All funds collected from Subscribers will be deposited in an interest bearing account held by the Company. Subscriptions will be deposited in a non-interest bearing account. All proceeds from the sale of the Shares shall, upon receipt and acceptance of the subscriptions, be disbursed to the Company in accordance with the "Use of Proceeds". The Company may also elect to retain an agent (the "Placement Agent") to offer the Shares on a "best efforts" basis. If all 500,000 Shares are sold, the Placement Agent will be entitled to 10%, or $50,000, of the total subscription amount. The Placement Agent will also be entitled to a non-accountable expense allowance equal to three (3%) percent of the Offering price ($.03 per Share).

(2)   The offer and/or sale of the Shares offered thereby will be conducted by Officers, Directors and/or agents of the Company who may receive commissions and/ or any other form of compensation for the sale of any of the Shares. The Company also reserves the right to engage members of the National Association of Securities Dealers, Inc.("NASD") as agents of the Company to place all or a portion of the Shares offered thereby. Although the Company has no understanding or commitments with any such NASD member at this time, the Company may pay commissions to such NASD broker/dealers in an amount equal to the 10% of the gross proceeds from the sales of any such Share(s) made by such broker(s) / dealer(s) and / or agent.

No one is authorized to give any information or to make any representations other than those contained in this Memorandum in connection with the Offering described herein, and if given or made, such information or representations must not be relied upon. This Memorandum does not constitute an offer to sell any of the Shares offered herein to any person in any state or country in which it is unlawful to make such solicitation.

THE SECURITIES BEING OFFERED HEREBY HAVE NOT BEEN REGISTERED UNDER THE SECURITIES ACT OF 1933, AS AMENDED, (THE "ACT") IN RELIANCE UPON AN EXEMPTION FROM SUCH REGISTRATION, WHICH DEPENDS ON THE FULL COMPLIANCE WITH CERTAIN TERMS AND CONDITIONS, INCLUDING THE FOLLOWING:

THE COMPANY IS RELYING (i) EXEMPTIONS PROVIDED BY SECTIONS 4(2) AND 4(6) OF THE ACT AND RULE 504, THEREUNDER, IN ISSUING THE SHARES TO ACCREDITED INVESTORS OR TO INVESTORS THAT THE COMPANY HAS QUALIFIED AS SUITABLE WHO ARE U.S. CITIZENS AND (ii) EXEMPTIONS PROVIDED BY REGULATIONS OF THE COMMISSION IN ISSUING SHARES TO PURCHASERS WHO ARE NOT U.S. CITIZENS, AS DEFINEDD IN RULES 902(o) OF THE COMMISSION UNDER THE SECURITIES ACT. WITH RESPECT TO SHARES ISSUED TO INVESTORS

WHO ARE NOT U.S. CITIZENS, REGULATIONS PROVIDE THAT THE SHARES MAY NOT BE OFFERED OR SOLD TO A U.S. CITIZEN OR FOR THE BENEFIT OF A U.S. CITIZEN PRIOR TO THE EXPIRATION OF ONE YEAR FROM THE CLOSING AT WHICH SUCH INVESTOR PURCHASED THE SHARES.

THE OFFERING PRICE OF THE SECURITIES HAS BEEN DETERMINED BY THE COMPANY AND BEATS NO RELATIONSHIP TO ITS ASSETS, NET WORTH, BOOK VALUE OR POTENTIAL BUSINESS OPERATIONS. UPON CLOSING OF THIS OFFERING, THERE WILL BE NO PUBLIC MARKET FOR THE SECURITIES OFFERED HEREUNDER.

(i)   THE SECURITIES ARE NOT OFFERED THROUGH GENERAL SOLICITATION, INCLUDING, BUT NOT LIMITED TO, ADVERTISMENTS OR COMMUNCIATIONS IN NEWPAPERS, MAGAZINES, OR THER MEDIA; (ii) THIS MEMORANDUM SHALL BE TREATED AS CONFIDENTIAL BY THE PERSON TO WHO IT IS DELIVERED, AND ANY DISTRIBUTION THEREOF OR DIVULGENCE OF ANY OF ITS CONTENTS IS UNAUTHORIZED; (iii) EACH INVESTOR WITH RESPECT TO THIS OFFERING; AND (iv) THIS OFFERING MAY BE MADE ONLY TO PERSONS KNOWN TO THE COMPANY, AND AFTER RESONABLE INQUIRY, SHALL HAVE REASONABLE GROUNDS TO BELIEVE FINANCIAL AND BUSINESS MATTERS THAT WOULD ENABLE SUCH PERSONS TO EVALUATE THE MERITS AND RISKS OF THE INVESTMENT. THE INFORMATION WHICH MUST BE SUPPLIES BY THE INVESTORS IN THIS REGARD MAY BE RELIED UPON BY THE COMPANY TO BE ACCURATE.

The Shares are offered in subject to receipt and accordance by counsel to the Company to prior sale and to counsel's right to reject any order in whole or in part and to withdraw, cancel or modify the offer without notice. In the event the subscriber is rejected, his check and his subscription documents will be returned immediately by the Company. The Shares shall only be issued upon receipt by the Company of certification that the beneficial owners thereof are United States Accredited Investors or meet the beneficial owner standards both as defined herein.

See "Suitability Standards".

TABLE OF CONTENTS

SUMMARY OF PRIVTE PLACEMENT MEMORANDUM

THE COMPANY

The following summary is qualified in its entirety by the more detailed information and financial states appearing herein and prospective purchasers should read the entire Private Placement Memorandum.

Harlem Office Supply, Inc. (hereinafter referred to as the "Company") was incorporated on May 15, 1992 and is located in the heart of Harlem community's bustling commercial center. The businesses located in the area are mostly small and medium sized businesses, government offices, schools and the general public. The business's copy center offers high volume copying, word processing, typesetting, offset printing and binding services.

Harlem Office Supply, Inc. competes successfully through the quality of its products and services which included free delivery for its customers in the store's primary market area. the Company has identified core items that are both price sensitive and in demand and carries those items on a continuous basis and at a competitive price. The Company's competitive advantage lies in its ability to provide personalized services to its local customers. This gives them the opportunity to spend money within their community, thereby contributing to Harlem's overall economic health. This important benefit has enabled Harlem Office Supply, Inc. to collect a number of letters of commitment from local businesses that represents $296,000 in future sales on an annual basis.

The Company's office location is 121 West 125th Street, New York, NY 10027 and to provide maximum convenience to its customers it is open seven days a week. Its telephone number is (212) 864-3597 and its fax number is (212) 866-4603.

THE OFFERING

USE OF PROCEEDS

The Company intends to utilize the proceeds of this Offering the (i) aggressively pursue expansion plans (ii) to accommodate the new sales represented by the aforementioned letter of commitment, (iii) to hire additional personnel as it becomes necessary to do so, (iv) to increase its current office and storage space and (v) for general working capital needs.

See "Use of Proceeds".

THE OFFERING

The Company is offering, on a best efforts basis, a maximum of 500,000 Shares at an Offering Price of $1.00 per Share.

SECURITIES BEING OFFERED

Common Shares, $.001 par value:	500,000 (1)
Common Shares presently outstanding:	1,500,000 (2)

FOOTNOTES:

(1) Assuming all Shares are sold, the purchasers herein will acquire twenty five (25%) percent of the Company's total number of then Outstanding Common Shares.

(2) Excludes the exercise of a maximum of 50,000 Common Stock Purchase Warrants to be sold to the Placement Agent and others participating in the Offering. All of these warrants are exercisable at a price of $1.25 per Share.

RISK FACTORS

An investment in the Company's Shares involves substantial risks and should be considered only by those who can afford to sustain a total loss and do not require liquidity in their investment.

See "Risk Factors'"

REPORTS TO SHAREHOLDERS

The Company will, in future, furnish it shareholders with annual financial statements prepared by independent certified public accountants as well as unaudited quarterly financial reports and such other corporate and financial information as the Company deems appropriate.

RISK FACTORS

The Shares being offered by the Offering Memorandum represent a speculative investment and involve a high degree of risk. Therefore, prospective investors should carefully consider the following risk factors, among others, affecting the proposed activities of the Company prior to making any investment therein, as well as all other matters set forth elsewhere in this Offering Memorandum.

RELIANCE ON MANAGEMENT

The Company will be heavily dependent upon the continued services of its President and CEO Dorothy Pitman Hughes. Dorothy Pitman Hughes will be assuming the principal responsibility for the review of new projects, prospective ventures and for recommendations to the Board, which exercises final authority over such decisions. The Company's success will be largely dependent on the decisions made by Ms. Hughes and any additional members of management. In the event that current and/ or additional members of management are not employed or retained and should their services for some reason no longer be available to the Company, the Company's operations and/or proposed businesses and/or endeavors may be materially adversely affected. Furthermore, the Company may depend on its ability to attract and/or retain additional qualified personnel to manage certain business interests. Competition for personnel is intense and the Company may have to recruit qualified personnel with competitive compensation packages, equity participation and other benefits which may affect the working capital available for the Company's operation(s).

POSSIBLE ISSUANCE OF ADDITIONAL SHARES.

The Company's Articles of Incorporation authorizes the issuance of 5,000,000 shares of common stock. The Company's Board of Directors has the power to issue sub-stantial additional Shares and the right to determine the voting dividend, conversion, liquidation, preferences and other conditions of the Shares with shareholder approval. Management presently anticipates that it may choose to issue such Shares to acquire business interests in the future, although the Company presently has no commitments, contracts, or intentions to issue any additional Shares. Potential investors should be aware that any such stock issuances may result in reduction of book value or market price, if any, of the outstanding Shares of common stock. If the Company issues any additional Shares of common stock, such issuance will reduce the proportionate ownership and voting power of each Shareholder. Further, any new issuance of Shares may results in a change of control or the management of the Company.

CONFLICTS OF INTERESTS

Officers and Directors of the Company may engage in other business activities similar or dissimilar to those engaged in by the Company. To the extent that such Officers and Directors engage in such other activities, the will have possible conflicts of interest in diverting opportunities to other companies, entities or persons with which they are or may be associated or have an interest, rather than diver such opportunities to the Company. Similarly, such Officers and Directors may bring to the attention of management situations or projects in which they might have vested interest. Such potential conflicts of interest include, among other things, the time, effort and corporate opportunity involved in their participation in other business transactions or activities. As no policies have been established for the resolution of such conflicts, the Company may be adversely affected should these individuals choose to place other business interest before those of the Company. No assurance can be given that such potential conflicts on interests will not cause the Company to lose potential opportunities. In addition, the Company may be subject to disinterested shareholder approval and consistent with statutory procedures, invest in a business or property from management or affiliates of management. In such event, the terms of such participation in a project, entity or venture may not be the result of arms-length negotiations.

COMPETITION
Other companies and individuals are engaged in the same nature of business as the Company and such business is competitive. Many of the Company's competitors will have greater resources, personnel, technical know-how, and financial capability than the Company. Accordingly, there can be no assurance that the Company will be able to effectively compete with its competitors.

NO DIVIDENDS ANTICIPATED
The Company's investment objective is long-tern appreciation. To the extent that any income is derived from the Company's operation, it is likely that will be used entirely to fund additional operations, investments and/or continuing working capital needs rather than be distributed to the Company's shareholders. Consequently, prospective investors should not expect that any income dividends will be paid to them at any time during the life of the Company.

CONTINUED CONTROL BY PRESENT SHAREHOLDERS AND MANAGEMENT
Assuming the sale of all the Shares offered, the Shares of common stock purchased by investors in the Offering will represent 25% of the Company's outstanding common stock, and the present shareholders will own approximately 75% of the Company's outstanding common stock. As the Company's Articles of Incorporation do not provide for cumulative voting, after completion of this Offering, the present shareholders will be in a position to elect all of the Company's Directors, appoint it Officers, and control the Company's affairs and operations.

See "Principal Shareholders" and "Description of Securities".

DILUTION
As a result of the sale of the Shares offered hereby, there will be an immediate substantial increase in the net tangible book value of the Company's presently issued Common stock, and an immediate substantial dilution to the investors in the offering.

LIMITED TRANSFERABILITY
The Company's Offering presented hereby will not be registered under the Securities Act of 1933 nor certain state securities laws in reliance upon the exemption afforded by Section 4(2) of the Act and Regulation D thereunder and similar provisions of state securities laws. The availability of such exemptions depends in part upon the investment intent of the investors. Furthermore, the Company has no present intention to make public or file information pursuant to Rule 144 of the Act; such intention of the Company may further restrict the transferability of the common stock. Accordingly, subscribers for the common stock may bear the economic risk of this investment for the indefinite period of time.

LIMITED LIQUIDITY

The Shares offered herein are done so in reliance on an exemption from the registration requirement of the Securities Act of 1933, as amended, allowed under the provisions of Regulation D, Rules 504. Consequently, the Shares contained herein are registered under the Securities laws of certain States an may only be brought, sold, resold or otherwise transferred as authorized within those specific States. The Company has adopted that certain Resolution depicting its intention to seek Federal registration of its stock and further believes at the time of such occurrence, its fiscal posture and other related items will permit the Company to qualify for admittance to a recognized stock exchange in order to expedite the efficient trading of its shares. However, the Company is under no obligation and there can be no assurance that either occurrence would take place nor can there be any assurance that the Company's fiscal posture or other related items will reach a stage that qualifies the Company for the listing criteria of these Shares on any recognized stock exchange.

RELIANCE ON ADDITIONAL FUNDING TO COMPLIANCE GROWTH PLAN.

The Company is in immediate need of cash for equipment purposes and working capital to cover cash flow difference and believes that the proceeds from the Offering describe herein, after payment of the expenses of the Offering, will satisfy the Company's capital requirements to profitably conduct it operations. The proceeds from its Offering, in the opinion of management, would enable the Company to engage its growth strategy and would, in and of itself, permit the Company to profitably continue operations. However, a secondary Offering of the Company's equity may be necessary as a means of gaining an additional infusion of capital and could occur in approximately twelve to twenty-four months, commencing after the successful completion of this Offering, and may be applied to continue facilitating the Company's revenues and earnings. However, there can be no assurance that a successful secondary Offering of the Company's equity and/or other method(s) of gaining sufficient capital infusion(s) would occur. In the absence of such occurrence(s), the Company may be unable to realize the forecasted amount(s) of unit sales and/or earnings anticipated within the time frames indicated and may require the Company to grow at a reduced pace.

POSSIBLE APPLICABILITY OF PENNY STOCK REGULATIONS

The Securities and Exchange Commission (S.E.C.) has adopted regulations which generally define penny stocks to be securities with a market value of less than ($5.00) dollars per share, subject to certain exemptions. The Company's Shares, assuming a trading market commences, will be subject to these rules that impose additional sales practice requirements on broker-dealers who sell penny stocks to persons other than established customers or accredited investors. Among the sales practices to be complied with include a special suitability determination of the purchaser, a written receipt of the purchaser's consent to the transaction prior to the execution and the delivery of a comprehensive risk disclosure document, also prior to the trade. These requirements may restrict the ability of broker-dealers to sell the Company's stock to some of their customers and may affect the ability of the subscribers to this Offering to sell their Shares of the Company's common stock should a market develop.

FOR ALL OF THE AFORESAID REASONS AND OTHERS SET FORTH HEREIN, THE SHARES OFFERED HEREUNDER UNVOLVE A CERTAIN DEGREE OF RISK. ANY PERSON CONSIDERING AN INVESTMENT IN THE SHARES SHOULD BE AWARE OF THESE AND OTHER FACTORS SET FORTH IN THIS MEMORANDUM AND SHOULD CONSULT WITH HIS/HER LEGAL, TAX AND FINANCIAL ADVISORS PRIOR TO MAKING AN IVESTMENT IN COMPANY. THE SHARES SHOULD ONLY BE PURCHASED BY PERSONS WHO CAN AFFORD TO LOSE ALL OR A PORTION OF THEIR TOTAL INVESTMENT.

EXECUTIVE SUMMARY

Harlem Office Supply, Inc. (Harlem Office Supply) is a small retail outlet that currently offers business supplies to small and medium-sized businesses in its area. This attractive and neatly kept store has enjoyed steady sales growth since its inception by offering top quality office products at reasonable prices as well as copying services to its corporate and individual customers.

Harlem Office Supply competes through the quality of its services, which includes free delivery for customers in the store's primary market area. (Deliveries to customers outside the primary market area are made by United Parcel Services.) Harlem Office Supply has identified core items that are most sensitive, and keeps these items close in price to the large chains. The business' competitive advantage lies in its ability to provide personalized service while offering its local customers a chance to spend dollars within the community and thereby contribute to the community's overall economic health. The incentive to spend dollars with a locally owned business has made it possible for the company to collect letters of commitment for future purchases representing $296,000 in new annual business. The Company plans to install an advances point-of-sale computer system that will make it possible to be even more responsive to customer needs and strengthens its marketing efforts throughout Federal Empowerment Zones and Enterprising Communities.

Having profitably served Harlem Office Supply since its inception, Dorothy Pitman Hughes continues to serve as the company's President and C.E.O. Ms Hughes has been an owner and operator of new enterprises for more than twenty-five years. Ms Hughes is an individual of tremendous energy and vision, and has developed considerable time to community affairs while growing her various enterprises. The company is further supported by the CPA firm Seidel , Kessler, Blum & Co., P.C. Sperber, Denenberg Barany, P.C. Attorneys at Law, and Reginald Oliver, President, On Target Information Services.

The Company's current market area is the uptown section of Manhattan, including Harlem, Washington Heights, and Inwood. The greatest concentration of businesses, and therefore the company's primary market area, is Central Harlem where Harlem Office Supply is conveniently located. The businesses located in the area are mostly small and medium-sized businesses, with a notable number of large institutions. The business plans to increase market penetration by continuing its extensive networking activities within the local business community. Market penetration is aided by the distribution of flyers throughout the company and catalogs at the store, during sales calls, and through direct mail. The store displays most of its inventory on the sales floor according to a company developed plan-o-gram.

The Harlem community is gearing up for a ten year advance toward major economic change and an improved quality of life. Harlem Office Supply plans to continue playing supporting role in the move toward economic stability. The Federal Empowerment Zone, which includes Harlem, will see the investment of $3.65 billion for the growth of business and job opportunities. The owner of Harlem Office Supply has long been involved in the movement that brought about the Empowerment Zone designation. While Harlem Office Supply stands to benefit substantially over the next ten years, the company's owner is one of many community leaders and business owners committed to seeing the Empowerment Zone become a rousing success in Harlem.

COMPETITION

The Company's direct competition consists of two small companies located the same zip code as Harlem Office Supply. University Student Supply is located at 1201 Amsterdam Avenue. The store reports annual sales of $200,000. Helen's Stationery, Inc. is located at 285 St. Nicholas Avenue and report and annual sales of $80,000. Neither of these stores enjoys a significant competitive advantage in variety of merchandise, purchasing power, pricing, or quality of service. Harlem Office Supply enjoys a higher profile location, larger selling space, and a greater variety of services. Harlem Office Supply may someday face a competitive challenge from a large office supply chain. Harlem Office Supply intends to meet this challenge with superior service and commitment to the community. The company is also exploring the possibility of some form of joint venture with a major chain and met with a major office supply chain in June, 1995.

OBJECTIVES

The Company's objectives are to expand its present operations in order to generate new sales and to house an increased volume of inventory in order to meet short-term demands. In addition, Harlem Office Supply plans to purchase a point of sale computer system which will enable the store to respond more quickly to customer needs and to keep better track of items in inventory.

EMPLOYEES

The company currently employs four individuals on a full time basis. The management team includes the CEO and President, Ms, Hughes, a business to business sales manager, a copy center manager, a walk-in sales manager and a controller who handles the company's banking and fiscal matters. The Company intends to employ additional personnel as the need arises.

CAPITAL REQUIREMENTS

According to the estimated requirements for the Company described herein, and based on what the Company believes are sound business assumptions, Harlem Office Supplies' current capital requirements are $450,000.

PRODUCT & SERVICE PLAN

Harlem Office Supply's products and services provide needed items to the small and mid-sized businesses, institutions, and the general public of Uptown Manhattan. Offering high quality, brand name products at reasonable prices, free local delivery, and the opportunity to access additional business services such as high volume copying, Harlem Office Supply is a convenient and reasonable priced vendor to its costumers.

PRODUCTS AND SERVICES

1. Harlem Office Supply carries over 25,000 inventory items including general supplies, office equipment, office furniture, and other business related items. Those in the Uptown Manhattan area can also benefit from the company's free deliveries.

2. The business's copy center offers high volume photocopying, word processing, typesetting offset printing, and binding services. The new equipment to be leased will increase the company's capacity to perform additional services such as color copying.

3. At the customer's request Harlem Office Supply will take over management of the company's supply cabinet and keep it permanently replenished. Harlem Office Supply will assess the kinds of supplies a company is using and recommend better products to improve its image and efficiency. With Harlem Office Supply as their supplier, customers need not have someone at their company to deal with these issues.

UNIQUE FEATURES

Harlem Office Supply is Uptown Manhattan's only full-service supplier of office products, business related items, and business services. Harlem Office Supply enjoys the highest profile location of any competitor within its primary market area and has the largest selling space. The company has recently put an 800 phone number in-place for the convenience of customers making inquiries or placing orders by phone.

MARKETING PLAN

INDUSTRY PROFILE

According to the U.S. Department of Commerce statistics, the aggregate dollar amount of manufacturer's shipments of many of the categories of office products offered by Harlem Office Supply, exclusive of distributor and retail price mark-ups, is approximately $38 billion annually. Sales of office products in the United States are made primarily through office products dealers. These dealers generally operate one or more retail stores and utilize a central warehouse facility. The industry is highly fragmented with only a few regional or national chains. Dealers purchase a significant proportion of their merchandise from office supply distributors who in turn purchase merchandise from manufacturers. Goods purchased at the distributor's wholesale prices are marked up to provide a profit to the distributor. Dealers usually offer credit items to their business customers. Harlem Office Supply is charged close to full price due to the lack of a credit line and the young age of the company.

CUSTOMER BENEFITS

Local area residents, businesses, and institutions benefit from Harlem Office Supply's offering of high quality products at everyday low prices. A further benefit is the knowledge that the customer is spending his/her dollars at a business owned by a community resident committed to hiring from the local community, providing opportunities for advancement, and entrepreneurial training.

TARGET MARKET PROFILE

The target market for the office products and business related services offered by Harlem Office Supply is the businesses and institutions located in Zip Code 10027, where the Harlem Office Supply store is located. Zip Code 10027 is entirely within the Federal Empowerment Zone. The area's approximate boundaries are from Fifth Avenue to the Hudson River, from West 117th Street to West 134th Street. According to Dun & Bradstreet the area is home to 504 services companies, 281 retailers, 81 companies in finance, insurance, and real estate industries, 57 wholesalers, 31 manufactures and 30 construction companies. Dun & Bradstreet also states that within Zip Code 10027 there are 92 community-based organizations, 40 colleges and universities, and 2 hospitals.

Beyond the aforementioned Zip Code Harlem Office Supply targets all businesses and institutions within the Federal Empowerment Zone, which covers all of Upper Manhattan and the South Bronx. The business has mapped information which identifies primary and secondary business prospects, and competitor business locations for the products and services offered by the Company.

MARKET PENETRATION

Currently, Harlem Office Supply achieves market penetration in two primary ways, through its high profile location and the networking efforts of the company's C.E.O. The store's West 125th Street location has recently seen dramatic improvement. A complete street reconstruction has been completed. With its brick paving, traffic lighting replacement and other improvements, this busy commercial hub has undergone a striking facelift. The location is at the heart of the 125th Street Business Improvement District which is responsible for the maintenance of the improvements, the cleanliness of the commercial strip, and the promotion of the District's businesses.

Additional market penetration is achieved by the distribution of catalogs at the store and during sales calls, the distribution of flyers throughout the community, limited direct mail, and limited advertising in local publications. The store displays most of its inventory on the sales floor according to a company developed plan-o-gram. The Company will double the size of its store by leasing the adjacent storefront, allowing the business to enhance the volume and variety of its inventory on display. A major change will be the company's $26,000 budget for advertising & promotion, or 4% of sales. This money will be used to increase the company's printing and distribution of marketing materials, expand the reach and frequency of its now severely limited advertising, and strengthen its ties and commitment to the community by being a sponsor of community events.

The company is presently looking to enlist the services of an experienced Marketing Consultant specializing in marketing strategies with emphasis on sales and distribution. In order to benefit from the services of such a consultant Harlem Office Supply has budgeted $12,000 in Year 1 of the Financial Projections. The company will begin its search for the best matched consultant by meeting with the small business consulting department of Arthur Andersen & Company and organizations of similar reputation.

USE OF PROCEEDS

After deducting underwriting commissions, assuming the payment of a 10% commission on all Shares offered and other expenses associated with the Offering, the approximate net proceeds available to the Company will be $45,000 if the maximum number of Shares are sold. The following is management's estimate as to how the proceeds will likely be allocated:

DESCRIPTION	MAXIMUM	%
Acquisition of Additional Office and Computer Equipment (1)	$100,000	22
Advertising, Marketing & Promotion (2)	$50,000	11
Leasehold Improvements (3)	$60.000	13
Acquisition of Additional Inventory (4)	$80,000	27
Retention of Additional Personnel (5)	$40,000	9
Working Capital Fund (6)	$120,000	18
Total	$450,000	100

FOOTNOTES:

1. The Company plans on purchasing additional computers and equipment in order to become more efficient and competitive. This additional equipment includes a point-of-sale computer system and its accompanying hardware and software, a Xerox copier and a high quality Edit Color Copier.

2. The Company intends to implement an aggressive advertising and marketing plan by increasing its current distribution of marketing material and in-store displays. It also intends to increase its advertising in local publications. The company will promote itself through sponsoring community events.

3. The Company intends to lease space in order to expand its present operations. Currently there is 1,364 additional office space located directly beside its present location which can be leased for $35 per square foot. The Company intends to enter into a lease contract for this space and remove the present wall between the two offices in order to create a larger store.

4. In Order to meet short-term demands the Company intends to purchase additional office supplies including general office inventory, art supplies, items for churches and business related legal forms.

5. As it grows the Company will need to acquire additional personnel to work in the store itself and for administrative purposes.

6. The Company will require approximately $70,000 to meet operating expenses during expansion and $50,000 as a Deposit for Credit which will be used to establish credit lines with manufacturers to be suppliers to the store.

As this Offering is being made on a "best effort " basis which permits the utilization of proceeds immediately as received, the Company will use such proceeds essentially in the categories set forth herein and in the manner best suited to maximize its primary mission and objectives. In the event that less than the maximum number of Shares offered hereunder is sold, the Company's ability to implement its present operations and proposed expansion could be materially adversely affected.

The following table provides information concerning Shares of common stock owned beneficially and of record by the existing Shareholders of the Company of April 30, 1997 and its relationship to the Shares of common stock to be sold pursuant to this Offering.

CAPITALIZATION

The following table sets forth the capitalization of the Company as of April 30, 1997 and as adjusted to give effect to the sale of all of the Shares offered hereunder.

	PRESENTLY OUTSTANDING	AFTER MAXIMUM OFFERING
Shareholder's Equity	$1,500,000	2,000,000
Common stock - $0.01 par Value per Share Issued and Outstanding: 1,500,000		
Issued and Outstanding After the Offering: 2,000,000		
Common Stock Purchase Warrants (1)	0	50,000

FOOT NOTES:

1. There are no Common stock purchase warrants presently outstanding. Upon the sale of all the Shares offered hereunder, there will be a total of 50,000 warrants then outstanding, exercisable for a period of one (1) year commencing May 15, 1998, at an exercise price of $1.25 per Share.

MANAGEMENT

Directors and Executive Officers:

The Directors, Executive Officers and Manager of the Company are as follows:

NAME	POSITION
Ms. Dorothy Pitman Hughes	President and CEO
Ronald Pierre	Business to Business Sales Manager
Kevin Williams	Copy Center Manager
Delethia Marvin	Walk-in Sales Manager
Alee Barnes	Controller & Office Manager

Each director serves until the next annual meeting of stockholders and until his or her successor is elected and qualified. Each officer is appointed to serve until the next annual meeting of the Board of Directors and until his or her successor has been appointed and qualified. The Board of Directors has no executive, audit option or compensation committees.

The Company's Certificate of Incorporation, includes certain provisions which provides that officers, directors and advisors of the Company will not be liable to the Company or its stockholders for monetary damages for breach of fiduciary duty as a director, except for liability arising from (i) any breach of the director's duty of loyalty to the Company or its stockholders, (ii) acts or commissions not in good faith or which involve intentional misconduct or a knowing violation of law, (iii) any transaction from which the director derived an improper personal benefit, or (iv) certain conduct prohibited by law.

MS. DOROTHY PITMAN HUGHES, PRESIDENT & CEO

Ms. Dorothy Pitman Hughes is the current owner and founder of Harlem Office Supply and has long been dedicated to creating economic opportunities within her community. She has a long and impressive history as a developer, organizer and director of successful enterprises.

Ms. Hughes is the founder and organizer of the New York City's Agency for Child Development which has supplied care for several million children per year since its inception and thousands of city jobs for residents of New York. She also organized the first Battered Women's Shelter in New York, providing a much-needed service as well as employment. Ms. Hughes has also founded and operated three successful day care centers and a public community workshop school on the West Side of Manhattan. At Columbia University she was employed as a substitute teacher and taught a course, "the Dynamics of Change" at the College of New Rochelle. She presently substitutes as a teacher at New York's City College.

Ms. Hughes has also served on various committees and task forces. She became a member of the Governor's Task Force on Rape and the Governor's Task Force on Human Services; she also served as a member of the Black Economic Summits under three Presidents of the United States. Ms. Hughes was asked by President Jimmy Carter to run a Midtown West Side Campaign Office for his election and has received numerous Awards and Letters of Commendation from President Carter, the late Vice President Hubert Humphrey and the late Senator Jacob Javits. She was also honored by Dr. Dorothy Height with a lifetime membership of the National Council of Negro Women and was given the Legacy of Dr. Mary McLeod Bethune. Ms. Hughes also spent three years on the University Circuit as a public speaker and teamed up with other female speakers such as Attorney Florence Kennedy and feminist Gloria Steinman.

In 1985 Ms. Hughes became the first African American Woman to own and operate an office supply and copy/printing company in the City of New York. She developed the needed services for the Upper Manhattan area and became one of Harlem's anchors in business. Ms. Hughes is a member of several organizations that provide support to the economic and social development of the country's inner cities, i.e., The National Black Women's Political Congress, Black Women Enterprises (BWE), the Harlem Business Alliance, Inc. (HBA), the National Council of Negro Women, the Stationers Association of New York (SANY), the Economic Committee of the Harlem Empowerment Zone and the DPH Entrepreneur-to-Entrepreneur Marketing Network.

Ronald Pierre has diverse experience in the office supply industry. He was previously employed at Bombay Stationery, NY. The positions he has held have included responsibility for store design, manufacturer representation, management of staff, and community relations. He also holds a Security & Law Enforcement Certificate from the State of New York. He currently directs the expansion of retail sales within the store.

Kevin Williams has eight years of diversified experience in sales, inventory purchasing and customer relations. He has two years experience in retail management in office supplies and copying services. He presently assists with the weekly planning of store operations, customers and managing staff.

Delethia Marvin spends most of her time at the Company on the sales floor handling customer relations, taking sale orders and operating the cash register. Ms. Marvin has been with the Company since its inception and has played a major role in its development.

Alee Barnes is a long respected member of the Harlem community and possesses the combined tales of a controller and an efficient office manager. She presently handles all of the Company's banking matter and fiscal concerns, and has provided distinguished service in the management of the business' cash flow. She also has over twenty-nine years of experience in financial management.

PRINCIPAL SHAREHOLDERS

The following table contains information as of April 1, 1997 as to the number of Shares of common stock beneficially owned by (i) each person known by the Company to own beneficially more than 5% of the Company's common stock, (ii) each person who is a director of the Company and (iii) all persons as a group who are directors and officers of the Company, and as to the percentage of the outstanding Shares held by them on such dates.

Name	Number of Shares	Percent
Ms. Dorothy Pitman Hughes	1,500,000	100%

DESCRIPTION OF SECURITIES

Common Stock:

The company has a total value of 5,000,000 Shares of its common stock, $0.01 par value of which 1,500,000 Shares are presently issued and outstanding. Upon completion of the sale of all 500,000 Shares offered hereunder, there will be a total of 2,000,000 Shares outstanding without effect to the potential exercise of the warrants sold to participating selected dealers.

Holders of the Company's common stock are entitled to one (1) vote for each Share owned. Shares of common stock do not have cumulative voting rights; therefore, holders of more than fifty (50%) per cent of the Shares voting for the election of directors can elect all the directors and in such event, the holders of the remaining Shares will not be able to elect a single director. Upon completion of the sale of all 500,000 Shares offered hereunder, the subscribers to the Company's Shares will not be in a position to elect any of the Company's directors or to control its affairs.

Holders of Shares of common stock are entitled to receive such dividends as the Board of Directors any from time to time declare out of the funds of the Company legally available for the payment of dividends. The Company has never paid, and does not anticipate paying, any dividends in the foreseeable future. Earnings, if any will be used to finance the Company's expansion.

All outstanding Shares of common stock are fully paid and non-assessable. Upon any liquidation, distribution or winding up of the Company, holders of Share common stock are entitled to receive pro rata all of the assets of the Company available for distribution to shareholder, subject to the rights of the holders of any preferred stock or secured debt that may then be outstanding.

Common Stock Purchase Warrant:

The Company has authorized issuance of 50,000 common stock purchases warrants to participating selected dealers to purchase an aggregate of 50,000 shares of common stock for issuance upon exercise of such warrants. Each warrant will entitle the registered holder thereof to purchase one (1) Share of common stock at a price of $1.25 per Share subject to adjustment, for a period commencing twelve (12) months from the closing dare of this Offering and ending three (3) years thereafter.

As long as any of the warrants remain outstanding, the underlying Common stock to be issued upon the exercise of the warrants will be adjusted in the event of stock splits, stock dividends, recapitalization, reclassification or similar events. If any of the foregoing occur the Shares reserved for issuance upon the exercise of the warrants will be increased or decreased to reflect proportionately the increase or decrease in the number of Shares of common stock outstanding and the exercise price of the warrant will be adjusted accordingly.

The holders of the warrants are not entitled to vote, to receive dividends or to exercise any of the rights of holder of the common stock until the warrants shall have been duly exercised and paid for and the common stock shall have been issued.

For the life of the warrant, the holder thereof are given the opportunity to profit from a rise in the market value of the common stock, which may result in the dilution of the interest of other shareholders. In addition, the Company may find it more difficult to raise equity capital if it should be needed for the business of the Company while the warrants are outstanding. At any time when the holders of the warrants might be expected to exercise them, the Company would probably be able to obtain additional equity capital on terms more favorable than those provided in the warrants.

Piggyback Rights:

If during the period commencing two (2) years from the date hereof, the Company shall register any of its securities for sale pursuant to a Registration Statement under the Securities Act, the Company will be required to offer the holders of the Shares the opportunity to register the common Shares without cost to the holder thereof, subject only to the managing underwriter advising the Company that the inclusion of such shares of common stock would not have a material adverse affect upon its ability to consummate the sale of the securities proposed to be sold by the Company.

Report to Shareholders:

The Company will distribute to its shareholders annual reports containing audited financial statements prepared by independent certified public accountants. In addition, the Company shall, from time to time, issue unaudited financial statements and corporate reports.

Nature of Securities Offered:

This offering is being made in accordance with and pursuant to the provisions of Regulation D, Rule 504, as promulgated under the Securities Act of 1933, as amended Pursuant to such Rule, the securities offered hereby will not be subject to any limitations on the resale thereof under Federal Law. Such securities will, however, be subject to limitations on resale imposed by the Blue Sky laws of the individual states in which purchasers of the securities reside. The Company intends to qualify its Shares for trading in those states, including New York, Florida Texas, California and New Jersey, where the Offering will be made, to permit post-offering trading. Although the Company will use its best efforts to qualify its Shares for after sale trading in the several states where the Offering will be made, there can be no assurance that any or all of such states will allow after sale trading or that if such trading is permitted, that a two-sided market will develop. Consequently, purchasers of the Shares offered hereunder may be required to hold these Shares for an indefinite period.

LITIGATION

The Company is not a party to any material legal proceedings and to the Company's knowledge no such proceedings are threatened or contemplated.

PLAN OF DISTRIBUTION

The Company is offering to sell up to 500,00 Shares prices at $1.00 per Share and 50,000 common stock purchase warrants with an exercise price $1.25 per Share, exercisable for a one (1) year period commencing from One (1) year after the Offering Date. The Shares are being offered on a "best efforts" basis and funds will be available to the Company upon the sale of the Shares. The Shares are being offered by the Company's officers, directors and/or employees pursuant to Regulation D of the Act. No sales commissions will be paid to the officers, directors and/or employees for the sale of Shares described herein. The Company has not entered into any underwriting agreement with any NASD broker/dealer(s), whereby the broker/dealer(s), acting on behalf of the Company as a selling agent, has agreed to make a public offering on the Securities offered herein. However, the Company may and/or plans to enter into Selling Agreements with licensed broker/dealer(s) to undertake the dale of the Shares on a "best effort" basis. The Company intends to pay sales commissions and/or non-accountable expenses, but in no event will such commissions exceed ten (10%) per cent and non-accountable expenses exceed three (3%) percent. The Company will indemnify all broker/dealer(s) and/or selling agents.

Certificates representing Shares purchased shall be registered in the name(s) of the beneficial owner(s) as it appears on the subscription agreement and mailed to the address appearing therein.

Each subscriber hereof shall be required to complete a subscription agreement and other documents. The subscription agreement indicates the number of Shares to be purchased by the subscriber, the aggregate Offering price and describes the terms of the Offering. The subscription agreement must be properly executed by the subscriber hereof and returned, at a subscription price of $1.00 per Share, to 121 West 125th Street, New York, NY 10027 with a check evidencing the purchase of the Share payable to Harlem Office Supplies Inc. A copy of the subscription agreement, properly executed by the Company shall be returned to the subscriber upon acceptance of the subscription.

SUITABILITY STANDARDS

PURCHASE OF THE SHARES OFFERED HEREBY INVOLVES A CERTAIN DEGREE OF RISK AND IS SUITABLE ONLY FOR PERSON OF SUBSTANTIAL FINANCIAL MEANS WHO HAVE NO NEED FOR LUQUIDITY IN THEIR INVESTMENTS.

The Company has adopted as a general investor suitability standard, the following requirements for each investor:

a. He/she is acquiring the Shares for investment and not with a view to immediate resale or distribution

b. He/she can bear the economic risk of losing his/her entire investment;

c. His/her overall commitment to investments which are not readily marketable is not disproportionate to his/her net worth, and his/her investments in the Shares will not cause such overall commitment to become excessive;

d. He/she has adequate means of providing for his/her current needs and personal contingencies and has no need for liquidity in his/her investment in the Shares and

e. He/she (or his/her Purchaser Representative, if one is utilized) has such knowledge and experience in financial business matters that he/she is (they are) capable of protecting his/her own interests in connection with is investment.

The Shares offered hereby will not be registered under the Act and are being sold in reliance upon the exemption from such registration provided in Section 4(2) of the Act with respect to "transactions by an issuer not involving a public offering". In order to establish the availability of such exemption, the Company may elect to rely on Rule 504 of Regulation D under the Act, which provided that an Offering made in accordance with all its conditions is deemed exempt from such registration. The number of investors in an Offering conducted under Rules 504 is unlimited, provided however, that each is either a suitable or an "accredited investor".

An unlimited number of subscribers who meet the standards specified in clauses (a) through (e) above, may be accepted by the Company as suitable investors for investment in the Common Shares offered hereby provided that each such investor has a net worth sufficient to bear the risk of losing his/her entire investment.

The Suitability Standards referred to above represent minimum suitability requirements for prospective investors and the satisfaction of each standard by a prospective investor does not necessarily mean that the Shares are a suitable investment for such investor. The Company may, in circumstances it deems appropriate, modify such requirements.

Such above described representations will be reviewed to determine the suitability of prospective investors and the Company will have the right to refuse a subscription for the Shares if in its sole discretion it believes that a prospective investor does not meet the applicable suitability requirement or the Shares are otherwise an unsuitable investment for the prospective investor.

Neither the Company, nor any of its officers and directors will act as Purchaser Representatives for any of the prospective investors in the Company and neither intends to retain or select and arrange to compensate his/her own Purchaser Representative to disclose to the prospective investor in writing any material relationship between such Purchaser Representative, or any affiliates, which then exists or is mutually understood to be contemplated, or which has existed at any time during the previous two years, and any compensation received or to be received as a result of such relationship. The rule further requires investors to acknowledge specifically, in writing, the Purchaser Representative as such. Each Purchaser Representative will be required to sign and complete the Purchaser Representative's Certificate annexed to hereto as an Exhibit.

EXPERTS

The financial statement included in this Memorandum, to the extent and for the periods indicated herein, have been prepared by the Company and not reviewed by a certified public accountant.

ADDITIONAL INFORMATION

Should any potential subscriber or his/her Purchaser Representative desire any additional information regarding the Company and its operations or wish to review any of the underlying documents, they may do so by requesting such mater from Ms. Dorothy Pitman Hughes who will seek to accommodate such request during normal business hours.

HARLEM OFFICE SUPPLIES, INC.
REGULATION D - RULE 504 EQUITY OFFERING - SUBSCRIPTION AGREEMENT

HARLEM OFFICE SUPPLY, INC., a New York Corporation ("the Company") has represented as follows:

1. Terms Of the Offering.

1.1 The Shares are offered on a "best efforts", 500,000 Share maximum basis for a period of three hundred sixty five (365) days, commencing on the date of the Disclosure Document (the "Termination Date"). All proceeds will be promptly deposited into an escrow account for this Offering. All Subscriptions will be made payable to "HARLEM OFFICE SUPPLIES, INC".

1.2 In the event the minimum number of Shares is not sold within the Minimun Offering Period, defined as the Three Hundred Sixty Five (365) calendar day period commencing upon the effective date of the Offering (unless extended), the offering will be withdrawn and the proceeds will be returned to Subscribers without interest and without deduction for commissions or expenses.

2. Subscription.

2.1 The undersigned (the "Purchaser"), intending to be legally bound, hereby subscribes for Common stock Shares (the "Shares") of HARLEM OFFICE SUPPLY, INC., in the number of Shares indicated in Section 15 hereof, at a purchase price of $1.00 per Share.

2.2 The Purchaser will deliver payment directly to the Company together with completed copies of all applicable Subscription Documents.

2.3 The purchase price will be paid in accordance with the above Section 1, "Terms of The Offering."

3. Representations and Warrants.
The Purchaser hereby represents and warrants to the Company as follows:

3.1 The Purchaser has been furnished and has carefully read: (a) the Disclosure Document relating to the Shares; and (b) the documents
and other materials which are exhibits thereto or enclosed therewith or otherwise made available to the Purchaser, and understands the risks set forth under the section captioned "Risk Factors" in the Disclosure Document.

3.2 The Purchaser understands that the securities are being offered and sold in reliance on a specific exemption from the registration requirements of Federal law.

3.3 No oral or written representations have been made or oral or written information furnished to the Purchaser in connection with the Offering of the Shares that are in any way inconsistent with the information stated in the Disclosure Document.

3.4 The Purchaser, if executing this Subscription Agreement in a representation or fiduciary capacity, has full power and authority to execute and deliver this Subscription Agreement in such capacity and on behalf of the subscribing individual, partnership, corporation or other entity for whom or which the Purchaser is executing this Subscription Agreement;

3.5 If the Purchaser is a corporation, the Purchaser is duly and validly organized, validly existing and in good tax and corporate standing as a corporation under the laws of the jurisdiction of its incorporation with full power and authority to purchase the Shares to be purchased by it and to execute and deliver this Subscription Agreement;

3.6 If the Purchaser is a Partnership, the representation, warranties agreements and understandings set forth above are true with respect to all partners in the Purchaser (and if any such partner is itself a partnership, all persons holding an interest in such partnership, directly or indirectly, including through one or more partnerships), and the person executing this Subscription Agreement has made due inquiry to determine the truthfulness of the representations and warranties made hereby;

[INITIAL _____]   Page 1 of 3

4. Acknowledgments. The Purchaser is aware that:

4.1 The Company has limited financial and operating history.

4.2 The Purchaser recognized that investment in the Company involves significant risks and the Purchaser has taken full cognizance of and understands all of the risk factors related to the purchase of the securities, including but not limited to those set forth in the Disclosure Document.

4.3 The securities have not been registered upon the Act but have been registered under applicable state securites laws and by reason of an available exemption from the registration requirements of the Act may be sold, pledged, assigned or otherwise disposed of.

4.4 While the Shares will initially not be listed on any exchange, a market for the Securities may not develop. Therefore, the Purchaser may bear the economic risk of the Purchaser's investment for an indefinite period of time.

5. Acceptance of Subscription. The Purchaser hereby confirms that the Company has full right in its sole discretion to accept or reject the Subscription of the Purchaser, provided that if the Company decides to reject such subscription the Company must do so promptly and in writing. In the case of rejection, any cash payments and copies of all executed Subscription Documents will be promptly returned (without interest). In the case of acceptance, ownership of the number of Shares being purchased hereby will pass to the Purchaser upon the registration of the transfer to the Purchaser by the Company of a certificate or certificates representing the Shares subscribed for, as further described in an exhibit to the Disclosure Document.

6. Indemnification. The Purchaser agrees to, and hereby does, indemnify and hold harmless the Company, its affiliates, the officers, partners, legal counsel, accountants and affiliates of any thereof, within the meaning of Section 15 of the Act, against any and all loss, liability, claim damage and expense whatsoever (including, but not limited to, any and all expenses reasonably incurred in investigating and preparing or defending against any litigation commenced or threatened or my claim whatsoever) arising out of or based upon any alleged false represention or warranty or breach or failure by the Purchaser to comply with any covenant or agreement made by the Purchaser herein or in any other document fiunished by the Purchaser to any of the foregoing in connection with this transaction.

7. Irrevocability. The Purchaser hereby acknowledges and agrees, subject to the provisions of any applicable state securities laws providing for the refund of subscription amounts submitted by the Purchaser, if applicable, that the Subscription hereunder, is irrevocable and that the Purchaser is not entitled to cancel, terminate or revoke this Subscription Agreement and that this Subscription Agreement shall survive the death or disability of the Purchaser and shall be binding upon and inure heirs, executors, administrators, successors, legal representatives and assigns. If the Purchaser is more than one person, the obligations of the Purchaser hereunder shall be joint and several and the acknowledgments hereunder contained shall be deemed to be made by and be binding upon such person and each such person's heirs, executors, administrators, successors, legal representatives and assigns.

8. Modification. Neither this Subscription Agreement nor any provisions hereof shall be waived, modified, discharged or terminated except by an instrument in writing signed by the party against whom any such waiver, modification, discharge or termination is sought.

9. Notices. Any notice, demand or other communication which any party hereto may be required, or may elect to give anyone interested hereunder shall be sufficiently given if: (a) deposited, postage prepaid, in a United States mail box, stamped registered or certified mail return receipt requested, and addressed, if to the Company, to the address given in the preamble hereof, and, if to the Purchaser, to the address set forth hereinafter; or (b) delivered personally at such address.

10. Counterparts. This Subscription Agreement may be executed through the use of separate signature pages or in any number of counterparts, and each of such counterparts shall, for all purposes, constitute an agreement binding on all parties, notwithstanding that all parties are not signatories to the same counterpart.

11. Entire Agreement. This Subscription Agreement contains the entire agreement of the parties with respect to the subject matter hereof, and there are no representations, warranties, covenants or other agreements except as stated or referred to herein.

[INITIAL _____]   Page 2 of 3

12. Severability. Each provision of this Subscription Agreement is intended to be severable from every other provision and the invalidity or illegality of the remainder hereof.

13. Transferability; Assignability. This Subscription Agreement is not transferable or assignable by the Purchaser.

14. Applicable Law. This Subscription Agreement and all rights hereunder shall be governed by, and interpreted in accordance with the laws of the State of New York.

15. Subscription Information.
(To be completed by the Purchaser)

Number of Shares subscribed for:
[a], at the Offering Price of $1.00 per Share.

TYPE OF OWNERSHIP (check one)

[ ]   Individual *(one signature required)*
[ ]   Joint Tenants with right of Survivorship *(both parties must sign)*
[ ]   Tenants in Common *(both parties must sign)*
[ ]   Community Property *(one signature required if interest held in one name,*
            i. e., managing spouse, two signatures required if held in both names)
[ ]   Trust *(please include instrument creating Trust)*
[ ]   Corporation *(please include evidence of authorization to purchase in form of*
            resolutions or Articles of Incorporation and By-Laws)
[ ]   Partnership *(please include copy of Partnership Agreement)*
[ ]   Custodian (UGMA - Uniform Gift to Minors)

Please print here the exact name(s) *(registration)* Purchaser(s) desire(s) for the Shares:

_____   _____
Name   Social Security Number

_____   _____
Address   Zip   Telephone Number

If the Shares hereby subscribed for are to be owned by more than one person in any manner, the Purchaser understands and agrees that all of the co-owners of such Shares must sign this Subscription Agreement.

IN WITNESS WHEREOF, the undersigned Purchaser(s) do(es) represent and certify under the penalties of perjury that the foregoing statements are true and correct and that he has (they have) by the following signature(s) executed this Subscription Agreement this_____day of _____19___

_____   _____
Name of Purchaser   Name of Co-Purchaser *(if applicable)*

_____   _____
Signature of Purchaser   Signature of Co-Purchaser *(if applicable)*

                                                      _____
                                                      Harlem Office Supply Inc
                                                      Representative

[INITIAL_____]   Page 3

Appendix B

Media References

DOROTHY PITMAN HUGHES, COMMUNITY ACTIVIST.

Throughout the last three decades Dorothy Pitman Hughes has garnered much media attention for her heroic role as a community activist. The references to the newspaper and magazine articles are listed in chronological order and can be retrieved from the archives of the various publications:

1981 Amsterdam News	"Day Care Program Attacked"
1984 Amsterdam News	"Women's Unit Organized by Dorothy Hughes Raised $30,000 for Jesse Jackson"
1993 Amsterdam News	"Closing the Gap: A Dialog with Women"
1994 Amsterdam News	"Dorothy Represents Harlem Business"
1996 City Limits	"Back to Old Neighborhood Empowerment Zone Out"
1996 People Magazine	"A Hollywood Story That Harlem Had First"
1998 Fortune Magazine	"A Bit of Wall Street Comes to Harlem"
1998 Amsterdam News	"Queen of Harlem Business Offers Public Stock"
1998 Essence Magazine	"How to Get Involved in Shareholding"
1999 The New York Times	"A New Momentum Along 125th Street"
2000 Harlem News Group	"Harlem Business Woman Builds Bridge to Wall Street"
2000 Newsday	"Ex President Celebrates a Year as Harlem Neighbor"
2000 Harlem News	"Unique Holiday Gift Ideas"
2000 Teamster Women Magazine	"Hughes Speaks"
2000 The Jacksonville Advocate	"Monitoring Black Community Divide"
2000 Library Journal "Economics by Ann Burn"	
2000 Dialogue	"DPH Whose Inner City is This "
2001 Black Book News	"Empowering Who?"
2001 Carib News	"Small Business Surviving Gentrification"

2001 Amsterdam News	"Harlem Business Woman Honored"
2001 Black Enterprise	"Empowering The People"
2001 Harlem News	"Dorothy Hughes Willing to Believe"
2001 The Network Journal	"Living Under Jim Crow"
2001 Amsterdam News	"Harlem Merchants Urge Party for Clinton Arrival"
2001 Amsterdam News	"HOS, Inc. First Harlem Business to go Public"
2002 Amsterdam News	"Wake Up and Smell the Dollars"
2002 Amsterdam News	"Hughes Named Woman of Valor"
2002 Dorothy Pitman Hughes Speaks to the Librarian Conference	
2011 Arbus Magazine	"Sisterhood In The Community"
2011 Folio Weekly	"Never Surrender Dorothy"

Appendix C

Media References Structure of HOS, Inc.

Many articles were written about the structure of the organization and how we went about putting the merger in place. Listed below are some of the magazines and newspapers following this merger and showing readers that dreams can come true:

1994 Amsterdam News	"Dorothy Represents Harlem Business"
1996 City Limits	"Back to Old Neighborhood Empowerment Zone Out"
1996 People Magazine	"A Hollywood Story That Harlem Had First"
Oct 28, 1996 US News and World Report	
1998 Amsterdam News	"Queen of Harlem Business Offers Public Stock"
1998 Essence Magazine	"How to Get Involved in Shareholding"
1998 Fortune Magazine	"A Bit of Wall Street Comes to Harlem"
1999 The New York Times	"A New Momentum Along 125th Street"
Inbox 2000	"Empowerment to The People
2000 Harlem News	"Unique Holiday Gift Ideas"
2000 Teamster Women Magazine	"Hughes Speaks"
2000 The Jacksonville Advocate	"Monitoring Black Community Divide"
2000 Library Journal	"Economics by Ann Burn"
2001 Amsterdam News	"Harlem Business Woman Honored"
2001 Amsterdam News	"HOS, Inc. First Harlem Business to go Public"
2001 Black Enterprise	"Empowering The People"
2000 Dialogue	"DPH Whose Inner City is This "
2000 Harlem News Group	"Harlem Business Woman Builds Bridge to Wall Street"
2001 Carib News	"Small Business Surviving Gentrification"
2001 Black Book News	"Empowering Who?"
2001 Harlem News	"Dorothy Hughes Willing to Believe"
2002 Amsterdam News	"Hughes Named Woman of Valor"
2002 Dorothy Pitman Hughes Speaks to the Librarian Conference	

About the Author
Dorothy Pitman Hughes

Beginning in the 1960's, Dorothy Pitman Hughes worked in the Civil Rights Movement and was a key organizer in groundbreaking movements for community controlled childcare and education, and "Alternatives to Welfare" programs and legislation, which took many out of poverty. In the 70's she spent several years on a University lecture tour with Gloria Steinem. In 1971 she co-founded the Agency for Child Development in New York City, which today cares for 700,000 children and organized the first battered women's shelter in New York City. She was also on the original *Ms. Magazine* Task Force with Gloria Steinem.

Dorothy broke the color line with the Miss America Pageant. She was the first African American woman to own an office supply store in the State of New York, and she continues to work to organize and educate about economic empowerment and ownership. She has been an advocate for women's rights, civil rights, and children's rights for over 45 years.

Dorothy currently owns the Gateway Bookstore in Jacksonville Florida, which has become a community gathering place where small business owners meet to discuss ways to stay afloat. On June 1, 2012 Dorothy renamed her bookstore "Obama Cares" as a vehicle to organize community residents and to help ensure their votes are counted and are not damaged at the polls.

With Gloria Steinem's help, she has started the Charles Junction Historic Preservation Society Community Gardens Project in Florida, with a vision to bring agricultural and economic independence to urban communities. The gardens will create jobs, educational programs and entrepreneurial opportunities, while giving people in need access to healthy food and greater self reliance. Her project has planted two gardens to date, and is working to introduce the concept and build more gardens in communities in need.

Dorothy has also worked on numerous committees for several presidential candidates, including: Hubert Humphrey, Shirley Chisholm, Jimmy Carter, Jesse Jackson, Bill Clinton, Al Sharpton and Barack Obama.

Dorothy is the mother of three daughters: Delethia Marvin, Patrice Quinn and Angela Hughes and two grandsons: Sean William Ridley and Devin Edward Batiste.

I'm Just Saying, "It Looks Like Ethnic Cleansing" (The Gentrification of Harlem) is Dorothy's second book. She is also the author of *Wake Up and Smell the Dollars! Whose Inner City is This Anyway!* (Amber Books). Dorothy continues to lecture on college campuses where she is invited to speak about childcare, abuse, community and political issues. For further information or bookings, email: dorothyhughes02@yahoo.com.